Robert Irwin

THE HOME INSPECTION TROUBLESHOOTER

**Real Estate
Education Company**
a division of Dearborn Financial Publishing, Inc.

While a great deal of care has been taken to provide accurate and current information, the ideas, suggestions, general principles and conclusions presented in this text are subject to local, state and federal laws and regulations, court cases and any revisions of same. The reader is thus urged to consult legal counsel regarding any points of law—this publication should not be used as a substitute for competent legal advice.

Publisher: Anita A. Constant
Editor-in-Chief: Caroline Carney
Acquisitions Editor: Christine E. Litavsky
Managing Editor: Jack Kiburz
Editorial Assistant: Stephanie C. Schmidt
Interior Design: Elizandro Carrington
Cover Design: Salvatore Concialdi
Illustrations: Bill Reid

Library of Congress Cataloging-in-Publication Data

Irwin, Robert, 1941–
     The home inspection troubleshooter / by Robert Irwin.
          p.   cm.
     Includes index.
     ISBN 0-7931-1091-2 (pbk.)
     1. Dwellings—Inspection.   I. Title.
TH4817.5.I78   1994   94-36679
643'.12–dc20   CIP

Contents

List of Figures

Preface

I'VE always wanted to write a book on inspecting a home. Since I was first involved in real estate (more than 30 years ago), I've been interested in how homes were built and what secrets were involved in checking them out. Over the years, I've bought more homes than I care to remember, and one of the most challenging parts of the purchase has always been going through the home, trying to discover any problems that might exist.

Just for fun, I kept a list (mostly in my head) of what to look for when checking the roof, the plumbing, the electrical system, the kitchen, the baths and so on. I've revised it as building procedures and codes changed. But the list has gotten so extensive that I thought I'd better write it all down. And once written, why not share it? There must be thousands of buyers and sellers who would like to uncover the same things I want to know.

This book is the result. In it, I've given you my "secrets." I've also talked with dozens of qualified home inspectors and asked them for their methods of inspection, and I've incorporated these as well.

If you are buying or selling a home and want a home inspection, I believe this book will help you get a good one. It does not explain how a home is built or how to build one (as I've seen other books on this subject do). Rather, it tells you what to check out in an existing home so you can decide whether there are problems and, if so, how serious. It also tells you where to go for help when you need it.

This book truly is a troubleshooter. With it, you should be able to quickly determine whether your home is in good condition and, if not, why not and what to do about it.

Introduction
Why You Need a Home Inspection

THERE are two people who need a home inspection: a buyer and a seller. (If you're a homeowner, it's also a good idea to have a maintenance check at least twice a year. See Chapter 16.) Buyers need a home inspected so they'll know what they're getting. The days of buying a "pig in a poke" in real estate are long gone. Today, buyers want and are entitled to know all the secrets of a property up front. If it turns out there are some problems, it is usually possible to get out of the deal or negotiate a lower price. (I'll have more to say about that in a moment.)

Sellers, on the other hand, need a home inspection for a different reason. Today, sellers in most states must disclose any defects or problems with the property they're selling. It's actually to the seller's advantage to do this because once done, there's far less chance an unsatisfied buyer will sue for rescission (reversing the deal) or damages. After all, if the seller tells the buyer up front about a problem and the buyer goes ahead with the purchase anyway, there's not much left to be argued later. Having the home inspected gives notice that the seller has made a reasonable effort to detect any problems—even those that he or she didn't know about. While the inspection won't guarantee the seller against later action by an angry buyer, it will buy a lot of peace of mind.

Thus, in today's market, a home inspection is performed in most real estate transactions. Buyers insist on it. Sellers see it as great protection in a litigious society. And property owners can use it to help maintain their homes and get some reassurance that the properties are safe and secure.

As a Negotiating Tool

One aspect of a home inspection needs some additional explanation. It can often be a negotiating tool useful to both buyer and seller. Let's consider the buyer's perspective first.

Assume that, as a buyer, you find a home you like. You make an offer and it's accepted. However, you stipulate in the offer that the sale is contingent on your approval of a home inspection. (In other words, if the inspection finds something wrong, the deal is off.)

The seller signs and a few days later, armed with this book (and at the side of a professional inspector, if you choose), you check out the property. The seller, by now, has given you a disclosure statement. But you discover that there are serious-looking cracks in the foundation, the perimeter fence is about to fall down and the home needs a new roof, none of which are in the disclosure. Now you should have a choice (if your sales agreement was properly worded, with a contingency agreement tied to the inspection): You can back out of the deal, or you can negotiate.

You call in a structural engineer and a contractor, who tell you that the foundation cracks, though they look bad, are probably minor. Chances are they won't worsen, and they're causing no problems now. You call in other contractors and find out it will cost $2,000 for a new fence and $12,000 for a new roof.

Now, well prepared, you meet with the seller and tell him that the roof will cost $12,000, the fence will cost $2,000 and the cracks, which may or may not be serious, have devalued the property an additional $10,000. The inspection has revealed $24,000 worth of problems.

The seller is not happy; however, he realizes that all the reports you've generated will have to be disclosed to any future buyers and that those buyers will probably be just as anxious to get some sort of compensation. So the seller shops around and finds another contractor who will do an adequate roof job for $7,000. He figures he can fix the fence himself for $500, and because of the cracks, he's willing to drop the price another $5,000. He now presents this counteroffer.

With this counteroffer, here's what the inspection has gotten you as a buyer:

- A new roof

- A repaired fence

- $5,000 off the price

Yes, you could negotiate for more, but even if you settle for this, it's not bad. In the days before home inspections, you'd probably have proceeded blindly and ended up paying for the roof and fence repairs yourself. Now, however, chances are–unless you're unlucky–you won't have to do anything except patch the cracks. Thus, the home inspection has been a great negotiating tool for you, the buyer.

For the seller, too, there are benefits. If the buyer had gone through the purchase and later discovered the undisclosed problems with the fence, the roof and the cracks, there might have been a lawsuit for the $24,000 or more. The buyer conceivably could have even insisted the seller rescind the deal! From this perspective, the inspection got the problems out into the open and allowed the seller to deal with them at a minimal price.

Thus, the home inspection is really a plus for both buyer and seller.

The Inspection

This book will explain how you can conduct your own home inspection. However, be aware that while you can learn a great deal about what to check, there will always be some things for which you'll need expert help. For that reason, my suggestion is that you use this book in addition to the services of a professional. The combination should get you an extremely thorough inspection. (Besides, how will you know whether you have chosen a knowledgeable inspector unless you know what he or she should be looking for?) Check into Chapter 18 for tips on finding a good home inspector.

A home inspection, in my opinion, is not an option—it's a necessity. Anyone who forgoes it in today's world might just as well drive down the road with his or her eyes closed. This book will help you see where you're going and get the deal you want and deserve.

The One-Hour Home Inspection

WHEN you inspect a home, time should not be of the essence. You cannot be rushed if you want to develop the right information. With that information, you can be secure in the knowledge that the home is in good condition, or that it has some bad features that need to be looked at, or that it's ready to be condemned and you should run away as quickly as possible!

Nevertheless, sometimes you don't have all day to conduct an inspection. Rather, you want to get right to the nitty gritty. Perhaps you're conducting your inspection in advance of a professional inspector. Perhaps you're aiding a professional inspector. The point is, you want answers to the right questions now!

If that's the case, read this chapter first. Figure 1.1 shows a cutaway of a typical house indicating areas to check as part of a home inspection. In Figure 1.2 you will find questions to ask and areas of concern. Admittedly, not everything is covered in detail, but a substantial amount of material is listed. Furthermore, if you have problems understanding what is being asked, you will be referred to a chapter that should clear up your questions.

The questions start with the outside of the home, then work inside. Take your time. You can easily finish this in an hour. Don't run through the questions too quickly; carefully answer them. As I said, if you don't understand a question or how to reach an answer, check with the referenced chapter.

Figure 1.1 Cutaway View of a Typical House with Areas To Check

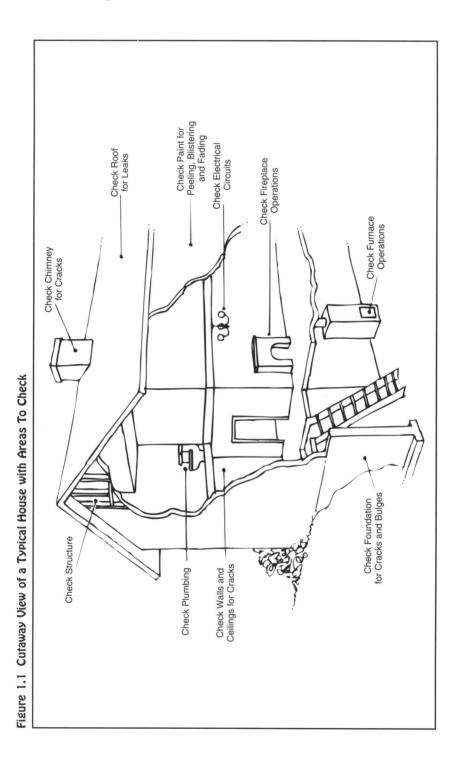

Check Chimney
for Cracks

Check Roof
for Leaks

Check Paint for
Peeling, Blistering
and Fading

Check Electrical
Circuits

Check Fireplace
Operations

Check Furnace
Operations

Check Structure

Check Plumbing

Check Walls and
Ceilings for Cracks

Check Foundation
for Cracks and Bulges

Figure 1.2 One-Hour Inspection Checklist

CAUTION—NEVER DO ANYTHING THAT COULD HARM THE PROPERTY. ALWAYS ASK PERMISSION OF THE OWNER BEFORE TURNING ON OR OFF ANYTHING OR ATTEMPTING TO POKE AT, PICK UP OR MOVE ITEMS.

Walk Around the Outside

Check the Site (See Chapter 3 for more details.)
- ❏ Is it badly located relative to the surrounding contours?
- ❏ Does it have poor exposure to sun and weather?
- ❏ Is the landscaping inadequate or poorly designed?

Check the Drainage (See Chapter 3 for more details.)
- ❏ Any signs of mold and wood rot?
- ❏ Any standing puddles or damp earth underneath the house?
- ❏ Any cracked dry soil underneath the home, indicating moisture at wet times of the year?
- ❏ Any water stains and efflorescence, indicating earlier problems?

Check the Foundation from Outside (See Chapter 4 for more details.)
- ❏ Any cracks?
- ❏ Any bulges?
- ❏ Any leaning or settling?
- ❏ Any other damage?

Check the Fuse/Circuit Breaker Box (See Chapter 8 for more details.)
- ❏ Is it adequate for the home (200 amp)?
- ❏ Is condition okay?

Inspect the Outside Walls

Check for Bad Paint (See Chapter 5 for more details.)
- ❏ Are all surfaces covered?
- ❏ Any rotting?
- ❏ Any chipping, peeling, blistering or chalking?
- ❏ Any stress cracking?

Figure 1.2 One-Hour Inspection Checklist (Continued)

Check the Metal Siding (See Chapter 5 for more details.)
- ❏ Any dents or scratches?
- ❏ Any bare metal showing?
- ❏ Are some pieces poorly joined?
- ❏ Any rusted nail heads showing?

Check the Brick Walls (See Chapter 5 for more details.)
- ❏ Are the bricks properly sealed against moisture?
- ❏ Any cracked or missing bricks?
- ❏ If painted, is the paint cracked, chipped or peeling?

Check the Stucco (See Chapter 5 for more details.)
- ❏ Any cracks?
- ❏ Any chipped, peeling or chalky paint?

Inspect the Outside Accessories

Check the Well (See Chapter 7 for more details.)
- ❏ Is well documentation in order (water quality, adequate pressure, depth and so on)?

Check the Pool and Spa (See Chapter 17 for more details.)
- ❏ Is operation okay?
- ❏ Any algae? Green, yellow, brown or black?
- ❏ Any faulty equipment?
- ❏ Any cracks or leaks?

Check the Outside Sewer System (See Chapter 7 for more details.)
- ❏ Is pipe condition okay?
- ❏ Are septic tanks and cesspool operative?
- ❏ Any odors or overflows?

Inspect the Roof

Check the Wood Shingle Roofs (See Chapter 6 for more details.)
- ❏ Any shingles falling off on the outside?
- ❏ Any tar paper showing through the shingles?
- ❏ Any evidence of leaking?

Figure 1.2 One-Hour Inspection Checklist (Continued)

Check the Asphalt/Fiberglass (Composition) Shingles (See Chapter 6 for more details.)
- ❑ Any leaking?
- ❑ Any mixed layers of shingles?
- ❑ Any shingles that decay or break easily?
- ❑ Any curling at edges of shingles?

Check the Tar and Gravel Roofs (See Chapter 6 for more details.)
- ❑ Any leaks and draining problems?
- ❑ Any areas of no gravel or shrinking (at the edges)?
- ❑ Any bubbling, curling or crumbling?

Check the Tile Roofs (See Chapter 6 for more details.)
- ❑ Any leaks visible from underneath?
- ❑ Any cracked tiles?

Check the Metal Roofs (See Chapter 6 for more details.)
- ❑ Any punctures and tears?
- ❑ Any discoloration, peeling paint or rust?

Check the Flashing, Gutters and Downspouts (See Chapter 6 for more details.)
- ❑ Any leaks, rust or cracks?
- ❑ Any separation from the home?
- ❑ Any rotting?

Go Inside

Check the Interior Walls (See Chapter 5 for more details.)
- ❑ Any scratches and marks?
- ❑ Any cracks?

Check the Floors (See Chapter 12 for more details.)
- ❑ Any squeaks?
- ❑ Any uneven floors?
- ❑ Any broken, scratched or loose tiles?
- ❑ Any rotten or soiled carpeting?

Figure 1.2 One-Hour Inspection Checklist (Continued)

Check the Security and Safety Features (See Chapter 13 for more details.)
- ❏ Any fire extinguishers?
- ❏ Any smoke alarms?
- ❏ What is the distance to the nearest fire plug?
- ❏ Any interior sprinkler system?
- ❏ Any locks?
- ❏ Any security system?

Check the Slab (See Chapter 4 for more details.)
- ❏ Any cracks?
- ❏ Any tilting or settling?
- ❏ Any separation from the peripheral foundation?

Check the Ground Wires (See Chapter 8 for more details.)
- ❏ Are they connected at all plugs, switches and outlets?

Check the wood-burning stove (See Chapter 9 for more details.)
- ❏ Any cracks, broken fire bricks, broken glass or loose or missing door insulators?
- ❏ Is the flue clean?
- ❏ Any approval sticker?

Check the Fireplace (See Chapter 10 for more details.)
- ❏ Does the damper work?
- ❏ Does it draw? Does it smoke?
- ❏ Does it have a spark arrestor?
- ❏ Any cracked bricks outside or inside?
- ❏ Any water leaks where it goes through the ceiling?
- ❏ Is the mantel sagging (check underneath)?

Go into the Bathrooms

Check the Faucets (See Chapter 7 for more details.)
- ❏ Any leaking?
- ❏ Any rusting or other pipe problems?
- ❏ Any overly low or high water pressure?
- ❏ What about the outside faucets?

Figure 1.2 One-Hour Inspection Checklist (Continued)

Check the Toilets (See Chapter 7 for more details.)
❑ Does the mechanism work?
❑ Any leaks?
❑ Any poor drainage (takes a long time to drain)?

Check the Tubs and Showers (See Chapter 7 for more details.)
❑ Any leaks?
❑ Any scratches and cracks?

Go into the Kitchen

Check the Garbage Disposal (See Chapter 7 for more details.)
❑ Does it go on?
❑ Any leaks?

Check the Dishwasher (See Chapter 7 for more details.)
❑ Does it operate?
❑ Any leaks?
❑ Any rusting?
❑ Is the overflow (located on the sink) clear?

Check the Ground Fault Interrupter Circuits (GFIs) (See Chapter 8 for more details.)
❑ Does it operate properly?

Go into the Attic, Basement and Garage

Check the Attic (See Chapter 7 for more details.)
❑ Is sunlight obvious when looking up through holes visible from the attic, indicating a roof problem?
❑ Are any old leaks visible?
❑ Are the pipes in good condition?
❑ Are the vents in good condition?
❑ Any insulation? How much? What kind?

Check the Pedestals in the Basement or under the Home (Supports for Home) (See Chapter 4 for more details.)
❑ Has the dirt eroded from under the pad?
❑ Is the pad tilted, cracked or otherwise damaged?
❑ Has the column lifted off the pad (or lifted the pad itself off the ground)?

Figure 1.2 One-Hour Inspection Checklist (Continued)

Check the Wiring (See Chapter 8 for more details.)
- ❏ What type is it?
- ❏ Is it adequate for the home?
- ❏ What is its condition?

Check the Telephone and Cable Wiring (See Chapter 8 for more details.)
- ❏ Is it well grounded?
- ❏ Is it properly located?

Check the Forced Air Heating (See Chapter 9 for more details.)
- ❏ Are the ducts located at floor level or near the ceiling (floor best for heat, ceiling best for cooling)?
- ❏ Is the ductwork in good condition?
- ❏ Is the fan motor clean, without squeaks and working?
- ❏ Are there holes in the heat exchanger?

Check the Electric Heating (See Chapter 9 for more details.)
- ❏ Is it adequate for the home?
- ❏ Any burned wiring?

Check the Circulating Water-Heating System (See Chapter 9 for more details.)
- ❏ Any leaks?
- ❏ Is the pump, motor or valves worn?
- ❏ Is the heater worn?

Check the Oil Furnace (See Chapter 9 for more details.)
- ❏ Is there adequate storage (500-gallon tank or more)?
- ❏ Any oil leaks?
- ❏ Any water corrosion?

Check the Hot Water Heater (See Chapter 7 for more details.)
- ❏ What is its age and size? Is it adequate?
- ❏ Any leaks?
- ❏ Any deposits?
- ❏ Is the safety pressure valve operational?
- ❏ Is it vented properly?
- ❏ Is it tied down (in case of an earthquake)?

Figure 1.2 One-Hour Inspection Checklist (Continued)

Check the Insulation (See Chapter 11 for more details.)
❑ Is the home insulated? Ceiling? Walls? Floor?
❑ Is the R-rating of the insulation adequate for the home?
❑ Are the windows and doors insulated?

Check the Earthquake Retrofitting (See Chapter 15 for more details.)
❑ Is there diagonal bracing throughout the home?
❑ Is the stud spacing no more than 16 inches on center?
❑ Is the foundation tied down?
❑ Is the steel roof tied down?

How To Read (and Write) a Disclosure Statement

THE rules in selling real estate have changed. It used to be *caveat emptor:* "Let the buyer beware." Today's real estate seller would more appropriately be warned, "Let the *seller* beware!"

Because of increased litigation, mainly by buyers who sued sellers (and won) over undisclosed defects in property, today's sellers increasingly offer to buyers a disclosure statement that puts down in writing any problems with the property. In fact, disclosure statements are rapidly becoming legal requirements in real estate transactions in most states.

For the Buyer

The disclosure statement is a wonderful document for both the buyer and the seller. For those purchasing, here is something that buyers used to dream about—a document laying out everything that is wrong with the property. Furthermore, if a seller leaves something off the statement and the buyer later discovers that the seller knew about the problem (or should have known) and failed to disclose it, the buyer could have the right to either sue for rescission (forcing the seller to take the property back) or sue for damages. Can you imagine getting something equivalent when you buy a car—a statement from the dealer or the seller telling you everything that's wrong with the vehicle?

Troubleshooter's Guide

The great danger and temptation for the seller is fudging or lying on the disclosure statement. For example, the home has a cracked slab, but it's covered by carpeting and there's little chance the buyer or the home inspector will notice it. Should the seller mention the defect and thus risk losing the deal or perhaps getting a lower offer?

The answer, of course, is disclose everything. Imagine that the seller does not disclose the cracked slab. On the day the buyer moves in, she rolls back the carpeting (planning on putting in new carpeting) and finds huge cracks in the concrete. Do you think that buyer will be happy? Do you think she will not call her attorney immediately? If you do, you're living in the past. On the other hand, if that same buyer dashes to her disclosure statement and discovers you've plainly recorded "big cracks in slab in living room, dining room and hallway," what can she do?

The rule for the seller is simple: Disclose everything—even things you don't know about but should! (Conduct your own inspection with a professional. See Chapter 18.)

For the Seller

For the seller, the disclosure statement is likewise a real boon, if handled properly. By disclosing everything that's wrong with the home on the statement, the seller puts the buyer on notice as to the property's problems and, therefore, the buyer has less reason to come back later and complain. That is the reason I always encourage sellers to list every possible problem and insist on an inspection to disclose problems they might not know about. Get it out on the table up front, and you reduce the possibility of problems later on.

What To Look For

When you, as a buyer, receive a disclosure statement, you should understand several things. First, because many sellers realize these days that to avoid problems later it is to their advantage to disclose everything up front, many disclosure statements include items that may not really be serious problems but that the seller has included to be on the safe side.

Second, there is no guarantee the seller is smart enough to realize that disclosure protects him or her. Therefore, just because a problem is not noted on the disclosure statement doesn't mean that it doesn't exist. You must be prepared to conduct a thorough investigation of the property regardless of what the statement says.

Third, sometimes disclosure statements are worded in such a way as to suggest there is only a tiny problem when, in reality, there's a huge problem. In other words, you must learn to discern the wheat from the chaff.

What the Disclosure Statement Looks Like

The actual disclosure statement will vary enormously from area to area. In some parts of the country, no official disclosure statement exists, and sellers need to procure one, probably from an agent. Always have an attorney check it over. A typical disclosure statement is given at the end of this chapter, along with comments on what to look for.

When To Read It

You should receive the disclosure statement before you commit to buying a property. Take time to read it before the home inspection, and bring it along during the inspection so you can investigate any problems noted.

In California, which probably has the toughest disclosure laws in the country at this point, a buyer has three full days to rescind the deal with no penalty (no loss of deposit) for any reason after he or she has received the disclosure statement. The buyer also often includes a contingency in the sales agreement specifically giving him or her the right to have a home inspection (within a reasonable amount of time—say, seven days). If the home fails the inspection, the deal is off.

Troubleshooter's Guide

Before we look at the disclosure statement more closely, keep in mind that this statement can offer you, as a buyer, leverage. For example, if it turns out the home has a bad roof or a cracked foundation or something else of consequence wrong with it, you can point this out to the seller and give him or her the alternative of fixing it or lowering the property's price accordingly. If it were me, I'd prefer the seller give me the lower price. I'd like to fix it myself, just to be sure the job is done right. On the other hand, if the seller fixes it, the cost can be included in the financing.

The Disclosure Statement

The disclosure statement can take a wide variety of forms. Figure 2.1 is a typical form.

We'll consider several parts of the statement so you have an idea of what to look for and how to read between the lines. It goes without saying, however, that you should carefully scan the statement, noting any check marks that indicate a problem. For example, in our sample statement, the first two items indicate leaks.

I always make a copy of the statement (so that I don't have to write on the original) and then use a yellow marker to highlight any answers that suggest problems. That way, it's easy to find them when I'm conducting my inspection. As I investigate the problems, I check them off. Let's begin by considering the leakage problems.

Figure 2.1 Seller's Disclosure Statement

THE FOLLOWING STATEMENT IS INTENDED AS AN EXAMPLE. DO NOT USE IT WITHOUT FIRST TAKING IT TO YOUR ATTORNEY AND ASKING HIM OR HER TO MAKE IT APPROPRIATE FOR YOUR STATE AND LOCALE AND FOR YOUR SPECIFIC TRANSACTION.

SELLER'S DISCLOSURE STATEMENT

(To be filled out by seller and given to buyer. Seller, use a separate page to explain any defects or problems with property.)

Water

1 Any leaks (now or before) in roof?   Yes _X_ No___
   Around a skylight; at a chimney, door or window; or elsewhere?   Yes___ No _X_
2 Was problem corrected?___*MOSTLY*___
3 How?_____*CAULKING*_____
4 By whom? _____*OWNER*_____
5 When? _'94_ By permit? _NO_ Final inspection when?_____
6 Does home have gutters?   Yes___ No _X_
7 Condition?_____
8 Does home have downspouts?   Yes___ No _X_
9 Condition? _____
10 Any drainage problems?   Yes___ No _X_
11 Explain _____*USES SUMP PUMP*_____
12 How corrected?_____
13 When corrected?_____
14 Is water directed away from home?   Yes _X_ No___
15 Any flooding or grading problems?   Yes___ No _X_
16 Any settling, slipping, sliding or other kinds of soil problems?   Yes___ No _X_
17 Any leaks at sinks, toilets, tubs, showers or elsewhere in home?   Yes___ No _X_
18 Public water? _X_ Or well?___
19 Date well pump installed?____
20 Low water pressure?   Yes _X_ No___
   Where? (IN MASTER BATH ONLY).

Figure 2.1 Seller's Disclosure Statement (Continued)

Title

21 Are you involved in a bankruptcy?   Yes___No _X_

22 Are you in default on any mortgage?   Yes___No _X_

23 Do you currently occupy the property?

                                               Yes _X_ No___

24 Have you given anyone else an option, a lease or a right
    of first refusal on the property?   Yes___No _X_

25 Does the property have any bond liens? Yes___No _X_

26   Can they be paid off without penalty? Yes _X_ No___

27 Any boundary disputes?   Yes___No _X_

28 Any encroachments or easements?   Yes _X_ No___

29 Any shared walls, fences or other such areas?

                                               Yes _X_ No___

30 Any areas held in common, such as pools, tennis courts,
    walkways, green belts or other areas?

                                               Yes___No _X_

31 Any notices of abatement filed?   Yes___No _X_

32 Any lawsuits against seller that will affect title?

                                               Yes___No _X_

33 Do you have a real estate license?   Yes___No _X_

34 Is there a homeowners' association to which you must
    belong?   Yes _X_ No___

35 Any current lawsuits involving the homeowners'
    association?   Yes _X_ No___

36 Any conditions, covenants and restrictions (CC&Rs) in
    deed affecting the property?   Yes _X_ No___

37 Any easements or rights-of-way over the property to
    public utilities or others?   Yes _X_ No___

Structure

38 Any cracks in slab?   Yes___No _X_

39 Any cracks in interior walls?   Yes _X_ No___

40 Any cracks in ceiling?   Yes _X_ No___

41 Any cracks in exterior walls?   Yes _X_ No___

42 Any cracks in foundation?   Yes___No _X_

43 Any retaining walls?   Yes___No _X_

44   Cracked?___ Leaning? ___ Broken?___

45 Any cracks in driveway?   Yes _X_ No___

46 Any problems with fences?   Yes___No _X_

Figure 2.1 Seller's Disclosure Statement (Continued)

47 Is home insulated?   Yes _X_ No___
48   Attic? _X_ Walls?___Floor?
49 Any double-paned glass windows?   Yes___No _X_
50 Is there a moisture barrier in areas below ground level?
                                                          Yes___No _X_
51 Is there a sump pump?   Yes _X_ No___
52   Where?_____ _UNDER PATIO DECK_____
53   Why?_____ _DRAINAGE IN WINTER_____
54 Is there a septic tank?   Yes___No _X_
55   Active?___ Abandoned?___ Filled?___
56 Connected to sewer?   Yes _X_ No___

Equipment
57 Is there a central furnace?   Yes _X_ No___
58   Forced air? _X_ Radiant/water?____
59   Radiant/electric?____ Other?_____
60 Any room heaters?   Yes___No _X_
61   Type?_____
62   Location? _____
63 Is there central air-conditioning?   Yes _X_ No___
64   Installed date?_____
65 Any room air conditioners?   Yes___No _X_
66   Location?_____
67 Is furnace room vented?   Yes _X_ No___
68 Is there a temperature relief valve on water heater?
                                                          Yes _X_ No___
69   On spa?   Yes___No _X_
70   On pool?   Yes___No _X_
71   Is the pool heated?   Yes _X_ No___
72   Any cracks, leaks or other problems with pool?
                                                          Yes _X_ No___
73   Explain_____
74   Other?_____
75 Any aluminum wiring?   Yes _X_ No___

Hazards and Violations
76 Any asbestos?   Yes___No _X_
77 Any environmental hazards, including but not limited
     to radon gas, lead-based paint, storage tanks for
     diesel or other fuel, contaminants in soil or water,
     formaldehyde?   Yes___No _X_

Figure 2.1 Seller's Disclosure Statement (Continued)

78   Is there a landfill on or near property?   Yes___ No _X_
79   Is property in earthquake zone?   Yes___ No _X_
80   Is property in flood hazard zone?   Yes___ No _X_
81   Is property in landslide area?   Yes___ No _X_
82   Is property in high-fire-hazard area, as described on a Federal Emergency Management Agency Flood Insurance Rate Map or Flood Hazard Boundary Map?
                                              Yes___ No _X_
83   Is property in any "special study" zone, which indicates a hazard or requires permission to add or alter existing structure?   Yes___ No _X_
84   Any zoning violations pertaining to property? (Explain separately)   Yes___ No _X_
85   Any room additions built without appropriate permits? (Explain separately)   Yes _X_ No___
86   Any work done to electrical, plumbing, gas or other home systems without appropriate permit? (Explain separately)   Yes___ No _X_
87   Does property have an energy conservation retrofit?
                                              Yes___ No _X_
88   Any odors caused by gas, toxic waste, agriculture or other sources?   Yes___ No _X_
89   Were pets kept on property?   Yes _X_ No___
90   Type?_____CAT_____ Inside?_____YES_____
91   Any pet odor problems?   Yes___ No _X_
92   Any active springs on property?   Yes___ No _X_
93   Any sinkholes on property?   Yes___ No _X_
94   Is property adjacent to or near any existing or planned mining sites, toxic waste sites or other environmental hazards?   Yes___ No _X_
95   Any real estate development planned or pending in immediate area, such as commercial, industrial or residential development, that could affect property values?   Yes _X_ No___
96   Any abandoned septic tank?   Yes___ No _X_
97   Is a home protection plan available to buyer?
                                              Yes _X_ No___

Figure 2.1 Seller's Disclosure Statement (Continued)

Reports That Have Been Made

Seller notes that the following reports have been made and are available to buyer:

98	Structural	Yes___ No _X_
99	Geologic	Yes___ No _X_
100	Roof	Yes _X_ No___
101	Soil	Yes___ No _X_
102	Sewer/septic	Yes___ No _X_
103	Heating/air-conditioning	Yes___ No _X_
104	Electrical/plumbing	Yes___ No _X_
105	Termite	Yes___ No _X_
106	Pool/spa	Yes___ No _X_
107	General home inspection	Yes___ No _X_
108	Energy Audit	Yes___ No _X_
109	Radon Test	Yes___ No _X_
110	City Inspection	Yes___ No _X_

Items That Go with the Property

111	_____	Yes _X_ No___
112	Window coverings	Yes _X_ No___
113	Floor coverings	Yes _X_ No___
114	Range	Yes _X_ No___
115	Oven	Yes _X_ No___
116	Microwave	Yes___ No _X_
117	Dishwasher	Yes _X_ No___
118	Trash compactor	Yes _X_ No___
119	Garbage disposal	Yes _X_ No___
120	Bottled water	Yes___ No _X_
121	Burglar alarm system	Yes___ No _X_
122	Gutters	Yes___ No _X_
123	Fire alarm	Yes _X_ No___
124	Intercom	Yes___ No _X_
125	Electric washer/dryer hookups	Yes _X_ No___
126	Sauna	Yes___ No _X_
127	Hot tub	Yes___ No _X_
128	Spa	Yes___ No _X_
129	Pool	Yes___ No _X_
130	Central heating	Yes _X_ No___
131	Central air-conditioning	Yes _X_ No___

Figure 2.1 Seller's Disclosure Statement (Continued)

132 Central evaporative cooler   Yes___ No _X_

133 Water softener   Yes___ No _X_

134 Space heaters   Yes___ No _X_

135 Solar heating   Yes___ No _X_

136 Window air conditioners   Yes___ No _X_

137 Sprinklers   Yes _X_ No___

138   Where?_____ _FRONT AND BACK_ _____

139 Security gates   Yes___ No _X_

140 Television antenna   Yes___ No _X_

141 TV cable connections   Yes _X_ No___

142 TV satellite dish   Yes___ No _X_

143 Attached garage   Yes _X_ No___

144 Detached garage   Yes___ No _X_

145 Water heater   Yes _X_ No___

146   Gas _X_ Electric___

147 City water supply   Yes _X_ No___

148 Public utility gas   Yes _X_ No___

149 Propane gas   Yes___ No _X_

150 Screens on windows   Yes _X_ No___

151 Sump pump   Yes _X_ No___

152 Built-in barbecue   Yes___ No _X_

153 Garage door opener   Yes _X_ No___

154   Number of remote controls _2_

155 Is the property equipped with smoke detectors?

            Yes _X_ No___

Items that are Specifically Excluded from the Sale

156 Lamps? _X_

     Where?_____.

157 Window coverings?____

     Where?_____.

158 Other Items?   Yes _X_ No___

159   Explain _____

         _____.

Figure 2.1 Seller's Disclosure Statement (Continued)

> 160   Seller is aware of the following defects or malfunctions and specifically draws buyer's attention to them:
>
> ____ SOME CRACKS HERE AND THERE, INSIDE AND OUT. NOTHING SEEMS SERIOUS. OCCASIONAL HEAVY RAINS PRODUCE PUDDLING, SOMETIMES UNDER HOME.
>
> Buyer is encouraged to make a physical inspection of the property and to employ the services of a competent inspection company to obtain an independent verbal and written report of the property's condition.
>
> Signed by seller and buyer

Leakage Problems

Checking for leaks in the roof, chimney and so on is covered later in this book (see Chapter 7 and elsewhere). However, because the owner has indicated that there are leaks and that they were not fully corrected, I would specifically ask when and where the leaks occurred, and I would want to see them (see also the last area on this sample form). I would write down the current condition of the leaking areas. Furthermore, I would get a competent roofer to check the condition of the roof. And I would also make sure that the leaks hadn't done any damage to ceilings or walls and that they hadn't caused dry rot.

Furthermore, it's always a good idea to assume that leaks are worse than disclosed. Some sellers will get it down on paper that the leakage is a small problem. If it later turns out that the problem is more serious than a seller thought (the whole roof needs to be replaced, for example), he or she can point back to the disclosure statement.

Plumbing Problems

Note that on the sample form, there is only one suggestion of a plumbing problem—low water pressure in the master bathroom. Why low water pressure in only one room?

Could it be that there are galvanized pipes in the home that are corroded and blocked, the blockage showing up in only that one bathroom so far? Could it be that the plumbing for that bathroom is not up to code? Could there be a leak in the line?

All of the above are possible answers to the problem. Check into Chapter 7 for additional items to look for. Also, you may want to have a plumbing contractor check out the property.

Title Problems

Note that "encroachments or easements" has been checked affirmatively. This could be something as simple as an easement across the back few feet of the property granted to a public utility. Or it could be something as serious as having a neighbor's home built on the seller's lot or having a right-of-way for a sanitation company across the front lawn. Much of this should be disclosed by the title insurance company, but I would also get an expanded explanation (in writing) from the owner.

Troubleshooter's Guide

If you are trying to buy a property that is part of an HOA involved in litigation, you may find that you cannot obtain financing or insurance on the property. To get around this problem, you may want to take all the pertinent documents to the lender or insurer in the hopes that it will find the allegations trivial and allow you to go ahead with the deal. Otherwise, you may need a statement from the current insurance company or even the owner saying that he or she will indemnify you against any loss—something both the insurance provider and the owner may be disinclined to give you.

Another potential title problem has to do with the fact that the property is part of a homeowners' association (HOA) that is involved in a lawsuit. Many properties these days have common areas, swimming pools and tennis courts, all run by an HOA. And today, as never before, these organizations are embroiled in law-suits.

What's important to remember is that if the HOA gets sued and loses, each member (property owner) might be held liable for the damages. That means that you must seriously investigate all suits and their potential risk to you. You could be buying into a disaster, or a lawsuit could be something frivolous and not worth worrying about. Get all the particulars, and take them to a competent attorney for analysis.

Foundation and Slab Problems

The owner has not answered yes to number 38, indicating cracks in the slab, or number 42, disclosing cracks in the foundation. However, cracks in interior and exterior walls and ceilings have been noted.

Now, it could be that the owner is just being overly cautious. Tiny cracks often appear in sheetrock, stucco and plaster as a building settles over time, and that could be all that has happened. On the other hand, bigger cracks are almost always the result of foundation and slab problems. Even though the owner hasn't detected problems, I would definitely be concerned about the slab and foundation. Check into Chapters 3 and 4 for suggestions on what to look for.

Drainage

Again, although not specifically noted, this property apparently has a drainage problem. The proof is in the fact that there's a sump pump located outside. That can mean only that water is getting under the foundation, and the pump has been installed to help move it away from the home.

Be sure to investigate the operation of the pump, the reason for it and whether the ground underneath the home is dry. Also, check for a cracked foundation, which could have occurred because of poor water drainage (see Chapter 3).

Hazards and Violations

Hazards and violations are important areas of concern because they tell you whether there are any problems exterior to the property, such as zoning violations or the threat of floods or earthquakes. If any of these items is checked, get down to city hall to find out what studies have been done and what regulations are appropriate.

In this case, the owner indicates that a room was added without benefit of a permit. This could be a serious defect because, at least in theory, the building department might at some future time require that the addition be brought up to code. This usually occurs if you subsequently add on with a permit and the noncode work is discovered. In some communities, a building inspection is required upon every sale to detect any such work.

Pet Problems

The owner notes that a cat was kept indoors. Is that a problem? I hope not, but it could be. If a proper litter box was not provided, the cat could have urinated on the carpet. When that happens, the carpet must be removed, destroyed and replaced by new carpeting.

How do you know whether a cat has abused the carpeting? The only test I've found effective is the sniff test. Yes, it sounds ludicrous, but I'm not above getting on my hands and knees and sniffing the carpet in the corners and around walls, particularly if I detect any sort of odor in a room.

You can also often detect the presence of urine in a carpet by closing up a room for a few days or using a wet rug cleaner. That usually brings the smell right out.

External Developments

A home could be the prettiest one on the block, but if the county plans to build a sewage plant next door, the value of that property will plummet. If you're buying, you need to know future development plans and the seller needs to tell you.

A check in the yes column of number 95 will alert you to any possible problem. However, you might also want to check with the local newspaper for information on the subject, as well as with the office of county records.

Reports

Any reports that have been filed on the property should be given to you. Even if the report was completed by a previous prospective buyer who did not purchase the property, that report should be handed over to you. A seller's failure to give you the report could be considered covering up a problem.

Check with a few local agents to see what sort of reports are usually done. For example, properties in flood zones will usually require a flood report indicating where the property is located in terms of the flood plain and giving the likelihood of flooding. You may not be able to get financing or insurance without such a report. If appropriate reports have not been completed, you may want to pursue them. The cost may be the buyer's, the seller's or a combination, usually depending on custom in the area, although everything is negotiable.

Items Included

Be very careful here. Be sure that everything you think comes with the home really does. There have been countless cases where the seller took lamps, appliances (even those that appear to be built in sometimes just unplug and come out), drapes and even carpeting (when it was not nailed down). If you want an item included in the sale, be sure it's listed on the disclosure statement *and* on the sales agreement.

A Home Warranty Plan

Finally, one last method of protecting yourself is to obtain (usually at the seller's expense) a home warranty insurance plan. These usually cover all appliances, including the furnace and heater, and may cover many structural areas as well. They can often be expanded to cover spas, pools and other accessories.

Home warranty plans normally require that the seller of the property warrant that everything is in good, working condition at the time of the sale. Also, they usually require a minimum payment (deductible) for each service call, typically in the $35 to $50 range.

When a seller hands a buyer a disclosure statement saying that everything is fine, a home warranty plan should be the buyer's next step. Even if there are problems noted on the disclosure statement, a warranty plan can sometimes work as a solution.

3

Site and Drainage Worries

FIRST things first. The home you want to inspect may be a wonderful two-story Tudor with dozens of amenities. Or it may be a gorgeous splitlevel with a marvelous family room and two fireplaces. Or it may have all sorts of other benefits that make it seem the ideal home.

But before you commit your heart—and your money—to a home, be sure about some of the inflexibles. Most problems can be fixed, but some problems, such as a bad site location, you can't do anything about (short of moving the structure). If the home is badly sited, you may want to reconsider and buy elsewhere or be prepared to put up with some annoying problems that can't be solved.

Bad Siting

Poor siting can be anything from having a windowless side of the home face a wonderful view to having the home located at the back end of a deep lot, far from the street. One builder I knew put a row of homes on a hillside in what was a former streambed. When it rained, the water ran down the hill, right through the lots and the homes.

There's really very little you can do if an existing home is badly sited, short of moving on with your search. That's why it's important to take time at the beginning of your inspection to make a site analysis.

How Can You Tell Whether the Home Is Badly Sited?

Every lot and home is distinct. However, all homes have certain things in common, including how they are placed on the land, their exposure to sun, wind and rain and their natural landscaping.

Begin by asking yourself the following questions:

- Is the home badly located relative to the surrounding contours?

- Does the home have poor exposure to sun and weather?

- Is the landscaping inadequate or poorly designed?

Location

If the home is located on a perfectly flat lot with no distinguishing features in the nearby landscape (such as a rise or fall to the land, a river or stream, a large commercial building and so on), you can probably skip this section and go on to "Exposure." Most homes, however, are located on some sort of slope or have some kind of landmark nearby, even if it's only an old stand of trees (see "Landscaping," below). What you want to check is that the home melds with rather than fights its environment. (Also, determine that the environment itself is not disadvantageous, as when homes are placed too near industrial or commercial building sites.)

Is the Home in a Depression?

Probably your first consideration is to be sure that the home is not situated in a depression (see Figure 3.1). If the surrounding land is higher on all sides, water won't run off (meaning your home will be wet in rainy weather), and you won't have much of a view of anything except tall slopes. This is not to say that the home should be located on top of a mountain. That usually means difficult access and exposure to bad weather from all sides. Rather, there should be at least one side of the lot that slopes down and away. Furthermore, the front of the home should face this downward slope to give you a view and accessibility. (If it doesn't, the front of your home will face an upward slope—not a very desirable feature when it comes time to sell.)

Figure 3.1 House Located on Top of a Hill and in a Depression

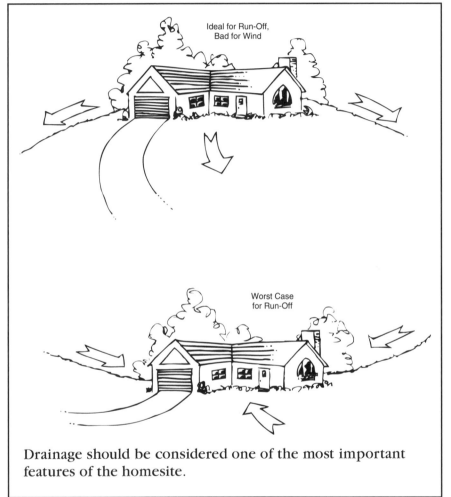

Drainage should be considered one of the most important features of the homesite.

Problems also can arise with homes that are built on the side of a hill. In a hillside situation, typically the upper slope will be at the back and to one side of the home, while the downward slope will be at the front and to the other side of the home. Check to be sure that the front of the home is placed in such a way that it faces the street clearly. The home front should be above street level. If it's below street level (so you walk down to your front door), it's a definite minus. Water will visit that front door in the rainy season.

Is the Home on a Cut-and-Fill Lot?

Another concern with hillside placement is the cut-and-fill lot. Here, the home is located on a hill. To make the original building site level, the builder came in with a tractor and cut into the hillside. The builder then constructed part of the home on the portion cut and part on the dirt taken from the cut and filled. The problem is that this often results in two different soil compactions—the cut part, which can be fairly solid, and the fill portion, which can be soft and might eventually sink. Cut-and-fill lots where the filled soil was not properly compacted may eventually settle on the fill side. Because the home often straddles the division between cut and fill, the settling of the fill portion can cause severe foundation and structural problems (see the next chapter on settling slabs).

You usually can tell the cut-and-fill lot by comparing it to the surrounding land contours. Typically, the hillside will slope down to about the middle of the building site instead of sloping all the way to the front. In other words, half the building site will be dug into the hillside, while half will jut out. Check for cracks in the foundation at the division between the cut and the fill.

Exposure

Does the home have a southern exposure? This is usually most desirable because the sun will hit the home directly, and most inclement weather (normally running west to east in the United States) probably will not. If most of the windows in the home face west, you might see great sunsets but receive little light in the morning. On the other hand, if most of the windows face east, you might see great sunrises and receive lots of light in the morning, but afternoons and evenings will tend to be dark. A lot depends on whether you're a morning or an evening person.

Homes near the top of hills tend to get more exposure to wind, rain, snow and so on. Homes near the bottom of hills avoid that but tend to get more water runoff.

Landscaping

You can always put in a lawn, shrubs and bushes. But can you plant a 40-foot tree? What about greenbelts behind or at the side of the home? What about ponds or cleared fields? These are all pluses that make a home more desirable, more costly initially and worth more on resale. On the other hand, you may actually want to deduct from a home that has no tall trees and no open or green areas nearby.

Deciduous trees planted close to the home (but not so close that their roots get under the foundation) are highly desirable. In summer, their leaves will shade the home from the sun. In winter, their leaves will fall off, letting the thin sunlight help warm the home. On the other hand, evergreens planted close to the home can actually detract from appearance and value, making the property dark and cold throughout the year.

Drainage

We'll talk about specific water-caused problems, such as cracking of the foundation, in following chapters. But for now, let's consider how water gets into a home and how to detect it.

Most water that gets into a home comes from runoff and poor drainage. Of course, there's the occasional case of an underground stream or an artesian well near the site. If that's the case, very little can be done, except for attempting to create barriers to keep out the water. Runoff, however, can often be deflected or carried away before it gets into the home and does damage.

When inspecting a home, look for the following in the basement or in the crawlway under the structure:

- Signs of mold and wood rot

- Standing puddles or damp earth

- Cracked, dry soil, indicating moisture at wet times of the year

- Water stains and efflorescence

Mold and Wood Rot

Mold and wood rot can cause decay and deterioration of the wood in a home. Left too long, they can completely destroy beams, flooring and other structural components. A competent pest inspection should reveal these problems. However, when looking for deterioration yourself, watch for black mold on wood. When you see it, push a screwdriver into the wood. Sometimes the mold is on only the surface and is harmless. But other times, your screwdriver will push into the wood as if it were soft cardboard. Wood in this condition has lost its structural strength. Also, look for yellow scum on the wood's surface. This can also indicate decay. (Check into Chapter 14 for information on termite and wood ant destruction.)

Moisture

Any sort of moisture or puddle in the basement or under the home is a bad sign. However, often the ground or the basement floor will be dry, particularly during the summer months. If that's the case, look for caking and cracks in soil. This is the sort of thing you'll see in a desert when a lake dries up. It's an indication of moisture other times of the year. You then must determine whether this is an old problem that no longer happens or whether it is a recurrent problem each rainy season. Recurrent wetting of the soil under a home can damage the foundation and slab, as well as provide an unhealthy environment.

Stains

On a cement floor or at the base of subsoil walls, look for water marks. These are often seen as brownish-yellow stains or sometimes, on concrete, as white stains. A white fuzz on concrete is called efflorescence and occurs because of the chemical reaction caused by water and the ingredients in the concrete.

Sometimes a seller may have washed and even painted the floors and walls of a basement so that in summer, no evidence of staining is apparent. You may want to move furniture, boxes or other materials stored on the floor and examine their bottoms. If they were stored there during the rainy season, they may reveal water stains, indicating a drainage problem.

Correcting Drainage Problems

Most, but not all, drainage problems can be corrected, often at a relatively small cost. If you can determine where the water is coming from, a drain tile (French drain) collection system can be laid across the flow (usually as deep as the lowest level of the foundation or basement) and the water can be directed around the home and out to the street.

On a site where the level of the drain tiles would be lower than the lowest level of the lot, a sump pump may be necessary. This is a simple pump that is set into a hole in the ground. It automatically turns on and pumps water up and out when the water level rises and turns off when the water level falls.

Troubleshooter's Guide

I recently installed a sump pump at my own home. I used a plastic garbage can with holes in it as the gathering spot. Then I sloped drain tile into the garbage can and installed a commercial sump pump (available at most hardware stores), with PVC piping leading out to the street. The total cost was less than $250.

Sometimes, in less severe situations, the drainage problem can be alleviated simply by more adequately ventilating the area, particularly in a crawlspace under a home. Most homes have ventilation openings cut out of the walls. Sometimes these are blocked and must be cleared. Other times, additional openings must be cut. It may even be necessary to mount an exhaust fan to clear out moisture. (The fan should be connected to an electronic moisture sensor so you don't have to check it all the time.)

Moisture Barriers

Finally, a wide variety of moisture barriers can be applied to subsoil concrete walls, particularly in basements, to keep out moisture. Ideally, these consist of heavy plastic and should be applied to the outside of walls and under the floor. Other types of barriers can be painted on the inside of walls as long as no significant hydrostatic pressure exists (no water pushing to get in, only moisture). In appropriate settings, these moisture barriers work quite well.

Checking Out the Foundation

THE foundation holds up a home. Quite literally, if your home has a bad foundation, it could fall down. More likely, however, a bad foundation means cracks will appear in walls, doors won't close properly and floors will be uneven. This condition could get progressively worse, lasting for decades, before there is any serious threat of the structure itself collapsing. Nevertheless, a bad foundation is a serious problem for any property and must be assessed carefully. It might easily be the reason that a buyer could demand and a seller could agree to a lower price, if not direct corrective work.

This chapter will troubleshoot foundations. We'll consider what can go wrong with peripheral foundations, slabs and concrete pads.

Peripheral Foundations

Most, although not all, homes have peripheral foundations of cement or brick. This simply means that the main foundation runs around the outside edge of the home. Of course, there may be additional foundation supports directly underneath the home such as a foundation wall, piers or both.

The biggest concern in peripheral foundations that are still in relatively good shape is cracks. Almost every peripheral cement or brick foundation has some cracks. These cracks often appear, in fact, almost as soon as the material is poured or laid. Most of them are harmless, indicating minor stresses. But some are much worse than others, indicating serious problems. The real trick in troubleshooting a peripheral foundation is to separate the harmless from the problem cracks.

Why Cracks Are Important

A crack in a peripheral foundation is like a crack in a car engine block. In a car, it means that fluids will mix, pressures won't hold and, generally speaking, the engine won't run properly, if at all. In a home, it means that the foundation, while still intact, may be slowly giving way, causing some minor cracks and other problems in the home itself in the meantime. More importantly, however, a crack in a peripheral foundation indicates more serious problems to come in the future.

Troubleshooter's Guide

It's important not to panic when you see cracks in a foundation. As we'll see, not all cracks indicate problems. Furthermore, even those that are serious may not indicate a condition that needs immediate correction. The cracks could relate to an old problem that has since stabilized.

Causes of Cracks and Other Problems with Peripheral Foundations

The single biggest cause of cracks in foundations is improper construction; they were built wrong to begin with. Usually, that means the foundations are not hefty enough.

When you look at the peripheral foundation of a home, usually you see only a small portion of it. A larger part may be underground. Indeed, the deeper the foundation, or footing, goes underground, the better. In areas where there is soil movement, underground water, freezing weather or expansive soil (the ground expands and contracts depending on the degree of moisture), footings that are as deep as 18 or 24 inches or more are not uncommon. The idea is to get down to solid ground. However, in some areas, there simply is no solid ground; therefore, the footing should be built hefty enough that it will support the home even on weak soil.

When building a proper foundation, the contractor will typically dig a hole—for example, 24 inches below the surrounding soil, perhaps 12 inches wide all along the periphery of the home. Then steel bars (rebars) will be run along both the bottom and the top (which will extend a foot or more above the ground) of the foundation, with vertical steel bars as additional support. Cement will then be poured around the rebars. (I can recall building a room addition where the footings were 40 inches deep and 2 feet wide! It used an amazing amount of cement and steel, and the laborers referred to it as a rocket launching pad. It was on expansive soil, and though the rest of the home's foundation has since cracked, to this day—nearly 15 years later—my room addition is rock solid.)

Cement and steel are an extremely sturdy combination and, if built hefty enough (deep, wide footings with a lot of steel), will support the weight of the home and keep it steady, even if the ground expands, contracts or moves. I have seen homes built (unwisely) near the edges of cliffs on the California coast, where the cliffs themselves have fallen away yet the homes remain intact, supported by hefty peripheral foundations. The homes' edges jut out into the thin air!

Sometimes, instead of cement, concrete blocks or bricks are used to build a foundation. These are normally not quite as good as steel and cement, but they're a close second. If rebars are used in the hollows in the concrete blocks and these are then filled with concrete, the blocks make a very strong foundation.

Causes of Cracks in Peripheral Foundations

Usually, peripheral foundations crack because the footings are not deep enough, are not wide enough or do not have enough steel. I have seen homes where the footings were only 6 to 8 inches deep. In this situation, when the ground moves, for whatever reason, the foundation simply isn't hefty enough to hold the structure steady. The pressure of ground movement and the weight of the home cause the foundation to crack and begin to deteriorate. In time, the foundation will break apart, and the home will collapse.

Although placing steel bars in cement and brick foundations is now required in building codes almost everywhere, I have seen construction in which the original contractor cheated and left out the steel, as well as old homes built before the codes required steel. Typically, sooner or later, these foundations break, and as the homes age, the two sides of the breaks go their separate ways. I've seen homes with dozens of breaks and the foundations leaning like tombstones in an abandoned cemetery. The wood in the homes may strain to stay on the foundations, but eventually it will come loose and the structure will collapse. Nothing short of lifting these homes and then repouring new foundations will correct the problem.

Where To Check for Cracks

One of the first areas you should scrutinize is the outside foundation wall (see Figure 4.1). Simply walk around the entire home looking at the cement or brickwork below the regular wall itself. Pay particular attention to any cracks, as well as any patches that might cover up cracks. I like to make a quick drawing of the basic layout of the home and indicate the location of cracks and patches on the peripheral foundation.

Figure 4.1 Foundation Showing Cracks and Bulges

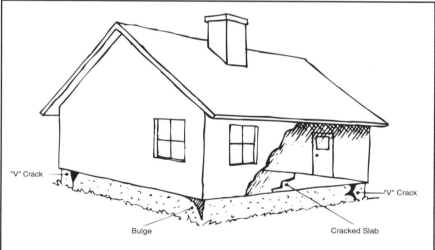

Foundation problems—"V" cracks are serious as are bulges and larger cracks in slabs.

The next step might be harder. Having examined the foundation from the outside, you must now look at it from the inside. If the home has a basement, that can be an easy task. If not, it may mean crawling underneath the home, where all the bugs, toads and beetles live. (I have an old mechanic's jump suit, a forlorn baseball hat and some old tennis shoes that I use for crawling underneath homes. You may want to use some throw-away clothes when you go under.) Of course, you could always leave this task to a hired inspector, but you won't know what's really going on unless you look yourself.

Troubleshooter's Guide

When you go underneath a home, check for many things at once. Don't consider only the foundation. Check the supporting beams for damage and termites. Check out electrical, heating and plumbing systems. Inspect vents, and look for signs of standing water. We'll cover all of these in later chapters. The caution here is to check them all at the same time. You don't want to go under the home more than once if you can avoid it.

When looking at the inside of the foundation, check out cracks and patched areas you noted from the outside. Often, an area patched outside by the seller or a previous owner won't be patched inside and you'll be able to see the crack more clearly. Also, you want to know whether the crack runs all the way through. A small crack on only one side of a foundation wall is usually nothing to worry about.

When troubleshooting a foundation, look for the following telltale signs:

- Cracks

- Bulges

- Leaning or settling

- Any other damage

Troubleshooter's Guide

I have an old contractor friend who claims—and I believe him—that he can walk through a home and, by the slant of the floors and how the doors close, tell you not only whether the structure has a bad foundation but where the cracks are in that foundation! Another of his techniques is to stand away from the home and look at where the roof line meets the top of the structure's wall. The line should be perfectly straight, with a solid meeting. If the line dips or separates, the problem probably isn't the wall or the roof, it's the foundation beneath.

Cracks   As noted earlier, small hairline cracks in concrete usually are nothing to worry about. Concrete itself normally cracks as it ages. If it encases sufficient steel bars, these cracks won't enlarge and, indeed, often are only on the surface. Any crack that is less than a 16th of an inch wide usually is a surface crack and shouldn't be cause for much concern.

V-cracks, on the other hand, are a different story. V-cracks can be anywhere, but they most often show up at the corners of homes, or, if the home was built on a hillside, on the downward slope at "steps" in the concrete. Typically, V-cracks start at the base of the foundation and may indeed be only a 16th of an inch wide, but as they rise up, they also open up and may be a half-inch or more wide at the top. Usually, they can be seen both on the outside and on the inside (under the home) of the foundation.

V-cracks indicate a broken foundation. The cement no longer provides structural support at the site of the crack. If there are rebars inside the concrete, they may be holding the two sides of the foundation together, although a widening crack often indicates that the rebars themselves either have broken or were never properly put into place. A large V-crack is the same as a broken foundation. It will only get worse, and at some point, expensive corrective action usually must be taken.

Corrective work may involve strapping the foundation on both sides with steel belts held in place by bolts drilled (not driven) through the concrete. In other cases, it may be necessary to dig shafts below the current foundation, excavate at the bottom, then pour a supporting foundation.

Bulges   Bulges can occur on any foundation but most often happen when cement bricks are used. They may indicate a compression of the bricks from the weight of the home and movement of the earth. This is particularly the case if the hollow core of the bricks was not filled with concrete and rebars. If you pry at the bulge, you may find that the surface actually is broken and that it comes away in your hand. Poking with a long screwdriver may indicate that the foundation itself has crumbled at the site of the bulge.

Corrective work usually requires removing the crumbled area and repouring a new concrete foundation at that spot.

Leaning or Settling   A foundation that leans inward or outward or sags downward should be readily apparent to the eye. You should be able to detect this from the outside of the home by standing back and viewing the foundation. A long contractor's level will confirm your sightings.

Leaning or settling usually, but not always, accompanies cracking. With or without cracking, you should suspect a drainage problem. Water may be getting under the foundation or putting pressure on it. Clay soil that expands can also cause this problem, as can earthquakes.

You have a variety of ways to handle a leaning or settling foundation, depending on the building codes in your area, the cause of the problem and the amount of money you can spend. Check with a contractor experienced in these matters. Keep in mind that in severe cases, it may be necessary to actually lift or at least support the home, remove the existing foundation and lay a new one—a very, very expensive proposition.

Slabs

In many areas of the country, particularly in the Southwest, instead of having a raised wooden floor, a home is built on a cement slab laid down on the ground. In other words, not only is there no basement, there is no crawlspace. There is only cement and then the ground.

Well, technically that's not correct. Properly built, there's a moisture barrier usually consisting of a heavy sheet of special plastic that goes between the soil and the slab cement.

Slabs are an efficient method of building a home. A great deal of expense is saved on wood flooring and on "cripples" (the short wall between the foundation and the first floor). In warmer climates, where there is no problem with freezing, and in areas where ground water presents no or a minimal problem, slabs can work quite well. Unfortunately, however, when a slab goes bad, it can mean big problems for the homeowner.

What To Look For in Slabs

Slabs tend to have problems similar to those of peripheral foundations (see Figure 4.1). Indeed, the usual technique is to pour a peripheral foundation and then to pour a slab inside it. (Technically speaking, the slab is part of the foundation, although most often, it is poured separately. The foundation is poured first, forming a sort of mold, then the slab with reinforcing steel bars or heavy steel mesh is poured inside.)

When troubleshooting a slab, look for the following problems:

- Cracks

- Tilting or settling

- Separation from the peripheral foundation

Cracks   As noted earlier, hairline cracks occur in almost all concrete and usually can be ignored. However, cracks more than about a 16th of an inch wide, particularly those running from edge to edge of the slab, are of particular concern. The slab itself is normally only 4 to 6 inches thick, and any distortion in the ground underneath will be reflected in serious cracks in the cement. Expansive soil, compaction of filled soil or erosion due to water can cause a slab to crack. Furthermore, a wide crack often indicates that the moisture barrier beneath the slab has been breached, and water could come up through the crack into the home.

Bad slab cracks often run long distances through the slab. They may be simple, such as a single wide crack (wide enough, for example, to put your finger through), or they could be offset, with one side of the cracked slab higher than the other.

Troubleshooter's Guide

Sometimes even moderate cracks in a slab can be safely ignored if the slab was properly poured with steel rebar. In some areas, the ground constantly expands, contracts or otherwise moves, and almost all slabs in the vicinity will have moderate cracks. However, the intact rebar holds the slab in place and prevents the cracks from widening and the two sections from offsetting. Check with a reputable contractor and inspector for advice on your area.

Locating Cracks You usually can't locate cracks in a slab unless you can see the slab. Floors covered with carpeting, linoleum, wood or other surfaces will hide all but the most severe cracks. To be thorough, you must remove the floor covering from the entire slab. Practically speaking, however, it is unlikely you'll be able to do this. So how do you detect the cracks? The truth is, in many cases, you probably can't. However, you may be able to get some clues in the following manners:

- Get down at eye level, and scan across the floor. Look for any linear bumps, distortions or settling.

- Check linoleum, wood or other hard flooring carefully. Sometimes cracks in the slab will come through these materials, at least for a few feet. Other times, cracks can be detected by a slight depression running across the flooring located above the crack. This can be hard to see unless you look carefully. Be prepared to move furniture if necessary.

- Check for tilting or settling, as explained in the next section.

- Ask the seller whether there are cracks. (If the seller fails to disclose serious cracks in the slab and the home has them, it may be grounds for rescinding the sale.)

Tilting or Settling Sometimes a slab or, more likely, a portion of a slab will settle or tilt. This may happen in homes where the building sites were cut and fill (see Chapter 3 for an explanation).

Usually, the soil on the cut hillside is more compact than the soil on the filled area (unless the builder properly compacted the fill dirt). The slab may crack at the division between the cut-and-fill area, sinking or settling on the filled side. Although unlikely, this can happen even if the peripheral foundation remains unbroken and does not settle.

The more severe the tilting or settling, the more obvious the problem. As noted above, get down on the floor and scan your eye across it. You should be able to detect any sunken areas immediately. If the floor is a hard surface such as linoleum or wood, roll a rubber ball or large marble across it. If there is a problem with the slab, typically the ball will roll slowly until it hits the depressed area, then pick up speed.

Separation   Ideally, when pouring the foundation, the contractor will leave small pieces of rebar extending into the area that will be filled by the slab. Thus, when the slab is poured, it has a solid method of adhering to the foundation.

Many times, however, this is not done, and the slab is free-floating. When this happens, the slab can ride up or down or even away from the foundation. To check for this, from the inside of the home, carefully examine the base of the outside wall and corners. Separation can often be seen as long cracks running where the slab joins the floor. I have seen cracks so wide that weeds were actually growing through them and into the home!

Note, a slab and foundation separation usually means that the peripheral foundation has at least one or two major cracks; otherwise, the slab would have no place to move.

What To Do about a Slab Problem

There are quick and dirty ways to fix slab problems, and there are expensive, long-lasting ways to do so. Quick and dirty often means just smoothing the edges of a crack with a cement cutter and smoother (especially if the crack is offset) then filling the hole with commercial plastic fill. This, however, is only a cosmetic fix. If the slab moves in the future, the crack, the offset or both will reopen.

If the slab problem is severe, in addition to determining the cause (water, ground movement or whatever), it may be necessary to pour a new slab. The easiest way to do this is to remove everything from the home, lay down a new moisture barrier and pour a new slab on top of the old one, assuming the peripheral foundation is intact. This, however, presents several problems. Besides the obvious mess it creates in the home, because the slab itself is 4 to 6 inches thick, the rooms will lose that much in height. This may require a variance from local building codes. Or, if this is not possible or practical, it may require that the home be jacked up and a higher peripheral foundation, in addition to the slab, poured.

Troubleshooter's Guide

I once owned a home with a number of significant slab cracks. I determined, however, that the cause of the cracking was poor rear yard drainage. Rainwater would run back toward the home instead of away from it. I put in French drains (discussed in Chapter 3) that directed all rainwater away from the home. This eliminated the cause of the cracking, and the slab stabilized. I then used a cosmetic approach to sealing the cracks. After nine years, they still remained closed. A big consideration here was that there was good rebar in the slab, meaning that without major ground changes, the slab was unlikely to move.

Needless to say, pouring a new slab is a very costly procedure, but if it seems necessary, consult with a contractor familiar with techniques used and acceptable in your area. Furthermore, if you suspect slab trouble, a contractor's written report may aid in adjusting the price of the property accordingly.

Concrete Pads (Pedestals)

Concrete pads are another part of a foundation. These are normally installed beneath supports that hold up the interior of the home. More commonly, look for them below the wood supports of a raised deck.

Troubleshooter's Guide

I can recall one horrible home that a friend owned. It was about 35 years old and had a slab in which the original contractor had omitted rebars. The ground was expansive, and the slab cracked in several places. Because there was no rebar to hold them together, these pieces moved up or down separately, and soon the floor of the home was offset here and there by as much as a half an inch. It was like living on a floor of large, flat stones, each set at a different level.

My friend valiantly smoothed the edges, filled in the cracks and attempted to stabilize the floor, all to no avail. The slab had a mind and a movement all its own. When he went to sell it, he advised potential buyers of the problem. As a result, no one would buy.

Eventually, it became clear that the only solution was to raise the home, put in a new peripheral foundation and pour a new slab. The retrofitting cost would be about $50,000. This compared with the cost of building a completely new home of about the same square footage for around $75,000.

Eventually, my friend abandoned the home. It went back to the lender, which sold it to a developer, which razed it and built a new home on the site. All of which is to say, never underestimate the problems a slab can cause.

Commercially available concrete pads are usually 8 to 12 inches square by about the same height. They normally have a wood block or metal holder on top that attaches to a wood column. They may also have a brick or cement pier placed on them. For light weight support, such as for decks, the pads may be placed directly on the ground. For heavy support, a hole may be dug and filled with concrete, the pad then cemented on top.

When examining a foundation—either for a deck or for a home—that uses concrete pads, troubleshoot the following questions:

- Has the dirt eroded from under the pads?

- Are the pads tilted, cracked or otherwise damaged?

- Have the columns lifted off the pads (or lifted the pads themselves off the ground)?

Erosion   Sometimes, particularly with external pads, water drainage will erode the dirt from under a pad. This is easy to see, as there will be a hole below the pad, which might not make full contact with the ground. This may mean the pad is simply hanging from the column instead of supporting it. This situation is usually easy to correct. You may need to jack up the joist above the column to make it level, then backfill under the pad with sand or concrete. The water that caused the erosion should be diverted. In more severe cases, it may be necessary to dig a hole under the pad and pour concrete.

Damaged Pad   Sometimes a pad will shift or crack, meaning that it can no longer support the weight of the column. This is easy to see. Correction is similar to that noted above.

Lifted Pads   Lifted pads are less common but do occur in a type of flooring that uses pads about every 4 feet, heavy inch-thick plywood on top and joists that are supported only by the pads and not by the peripheral foundation. Sometimes ground shifting will cause the flooring to buckle. This can be detected by raised areas on the floor above, as well as by columns that raise up, often taking their pads with them.

Correcting this problem is more difficult because it requires leveling the floor. This may mean shimming up pads, as well as cutting into supports in other areas. It usually must be done by a contractor experienced in the field. An entire home normally can be leveled for several thousand dollars.

Keep in mind that most homes have quite good foundations. Even homes that have some cracks in or other problems with the foundation often can have these corrected at minimal cost. It's rare that a home will have severe problems that are very costly, but it does happen.

Troubleshooter's Guide

The standard response by sellers to questions about foundation cracks and other problems seems to be, "It's been that way as long as we've lived here. If it hasn't changed over the past ten years, I doubt it will change much in the future."

Frequently, this homey assessment is correct if the cause of the problem (such as bad water drainage) has been alleviated. On the other hand, if the cause of the problem remains, the problem can only get worse.

When in doubt, call in an expert. Don't second guess. Severe foundation problems can get worse faster than you can imagine and can cost a fortune to fix.

Figure 4.2 Foundation Troubleshooting

Peripheral Foundation

❏ Any V-cracks?

Location _____ Max. width _____

Location _____ Max. width _____

Location _____ Max. width _____

❏ Any bulges?

Location _____

Location _____

Location _____

❏ Is the peripheral foundation leaning or settling?

Location _____

Location _____

Location _____

❏ Any other damage?

Slab

❏ Any cracks in the slab?

Location _____ Max. width _____

   Offset?___

Location _____ Max. width _____

   Offset?___

Location _____ Max. width _____

   Offset?___

❏ Is slab tilting or settling? (Apply rolling ball test.)

Location _____ Size_____

   Severity _____

Location _____ Size_____

   Severity _____

Location _____ Size_____

   Severity _____

❏ Is the slab separated from the peripheral foundation?

Location _____ Max. width _____

Location _____ Max. width _____

Location _____ Max. width _____

Cement Pads

❏ Has the dirt eroded from under any pad?

Location _____ Amount _____

Location _____ Amount _____

Location _____ Amount _____

Figure 4.2 Foundation Troubleshooting (Continued)

❏ Is any pad tilted, cracked or otherwise damaged?
   Location _____
   Location _____
   Location _____
❏ Has the column lifted off any pad (or lifted the pad itself
   off the ground)?
   Location _____
   Location _____
   Location _____

5

Locating Bad Paint and Wood Rot

THE face that a home presents to the world is composed of its exterior material (usually one of four types: wood, metal siding, brick or stucco) and the paint that goes on top of it. Inside, the walls are usually made of plasterboard (sheetrock), lath and plaster, or wood and, again, the paint (or stain) on top. By carefully examining the paint coat, you can often determine not only whether the home needs cosmetic work but also whether there's an underlying problem.

When inspecting, therefore, it's important to take the time to look at both the outside and the inside paint. Check several places on several walls. You can learn a lot with just your eyes and a screwdriver for poking.

Exterior

Let's begin with a word about exterior paints. What makes paint suitable for use on the outside of a home, among other ingredients, is a fungicide that's included in the mixture. This helps to ensure that mold won't rot through the paint. Indeed, I've seen paint that remained bright, stubbornly clinging to a moldy board.

What ruins paint, and may reveal problems beneath, are two things: moisture and poor application. Moisture is the breeding ground for fungus that can destroy wood and severely damage a home. A bad application of paint, even if the paint itself is first quality, may allow that moisture to get in.

Wood Siding

Wood siding is probably the most common exterior material found on homes. It can simply be plywood nailed on the studs. Or it may be in the form of slats or even shingles. If plywood is used, it is typically nailed on each stud, with the nails being no more than 6 inches apart. This provides both wall covering and diagonal bracing. (Bracing at a diagonal is vital in earthquake and hurricane areas to keep a home from collapsing under stress. See Chapter 15.)

When inspecting a home's wood siding, look for the following:

- Good covering of paint

- Rotting

- Chipping, peeling, blistering and chalking

- Stress cracking

Good Covering   All wood siding should be painted or stained. If it's left in its natural state, weathering will cause the wood to quickly warp, split and lift. Without proper paint or stain, a wood exterior can deteriorate severely within just five years. With proper protection, however, it can last the lifetime of the home.

To determine whether the paint or stain is covering properly, run your hand over the wood. (By the way, paint covers the wood, so you can no longer see the surface. Stain usually sinks into the wood but allows you to see the grain clearly. Stain can be either transparent or opaque.) The surface should be smooth. If it's rough, with little pieces of wood lifting and separating, either the paint or the stain probably is old and has deteriorated to the point where it is letting in moisture, which is ruining the wood. It is also possible that the paint or stain was not applied correctly (usually too diluted or insufficient in its coverage).

Troubleshooter's Guide

Don't always assume that damage to a wall from moisture occurs from the outside. Sometimes moisture will come from the inside. I once owned a home on a hillside where the downhill portion had a shingle covering while the uphill portion was part of a basement. Moisture seeped in from the uphill portion of the basement and seeped out the downhill side, causing the paint to deteriorate and the wood to rot. A well-built home will have a moisture barrier (usually a synthetic plastic material but sometimes tar paper) between the outside sheathing and the studs.

Also, check at the corners and the tops and bottoms of the siding. All of the joining pieces should have a solid covering of paint. If not, moisture can get inside. Note that all external wood should be above ground level, usually 6 to 12 inches. Wherever wood touches the ground, you have a strong potential for rot and termites.

Rotting   Dry rot is a problem, although strictly speaking, wood does not rot when it's dry. Moisture is the culprit. (There are termites and ants that attack dry wood, leaving behind a residue that looks like rot, but that's a different story. See Chapter 14.)

When wood gets wet, as when the surface coating of stain or paint breaks down and lets moisture through, fungus can gain a toehold. (There seem to be fungus spores everywhere just looking for a nice place to settle down and set up shop.) But even when wood gets wet, if it is allowed to dry quickly, fungus won't have a chance to get started. It's only when wood remains moist for long periods of time that rot occurs.

Any time you see a disturbance in the surface of wood, suspect dry rot. This is particularly the case at corners and edges. Take your screwdriver, and poke the suspected wood. Good wood will not yield, even to fairly hard pokes. Rotted wood will allow the blade of the screwdriver to penetrate and may even ooze droplets of water.

If a piece of wood is rotted, the rotted portion must be replaced. It's usually not sufficient to simply sand down the wood because rot penetrates deeply, destroying the wood. This does not mean, however, that if only one end of a board has rotted, the entire piece must be replaced. It may be possible to replace only the rotted portion.

Troubleshooter's Guide

Decks are a special problem. Often decks are so close to the ground that moisture builds up underneath them, then has nowhere to go. The biggest single problem with wood decks is usually that the deck planks are placed too close together. In dry weather, a good deck's planks will be at least a quarter-inch apart. (The boards usually swell up in wet weather, leaving less than an eighth of an inch space between them.) When the boards are too close together, they swell shut, and rainwater can't evaporate out. Instead, it rises and adheres to the bottom of the deck as moisture—and it stays there.

I once saw a redwood deck (usually renowned for its longevity) that was less than five years old yet was completely destroyed by wood rot. When laid, the planks had been placed directly next to each other and the ends of the deck had been sealed. There was no way for moisture that had risen from the ground during rainy weather to get out.

Chipping, Peeling, Blistering and Chalking   There may be other conditions affecting painted wood that do not directly indicate wood rot beneath. Sometimes wood will blister and peel. This is an indication of moisture but not necessarily of rot. Sometimes the wood was wet when it was painted. If that's the case, it's almost a certainty that there will be some blistering and, when the blisters break, some peeling.

Other times, all of the wood may not have been sealed. This is often the case with trim, when the flat front has been carefully painted but the edges have not. Moisture seeps in through the edges of the wood, eventually blistering or peeling it.

Chipping is actually a form of peeling. Here, however, small chips of paint will fleck away instead of peel away. The cause is the same.

For blistering, peeling and chipping, where there is no wood rot beneath, removal of the old, loose paint and application of a good sealer and new paint is usually the remedy. Often this may entail only one wall or one side of a home and need not be terribly expensive.

Chalking normally occurs on walls that have been painted with an oil-based paint. Over the years, the oil has dried out, due to weathering. If you pass your hand over the surface, it will come away with a chalky coating.

Chalking is not usually considered a serious problem. The chalk can be removed using a high-pressure water hose. However, using the high-pressure hose may also knock lose some paint. And it usually will not restore the old paint to its former brightness and color.

Stress Cracking   Finally, there is the matter of cracking. Harmless cracking usually takes the form of a series of tiny cracks that looks like the pattern on the back of an alligator. This often occurs in the middle of a wall, where the paint finish is supposed to look flat. It usually is caused when a second (or third) coat of paint is applied before the original is dry. Also, it sometimes occurs if paint of poor quality is applied during a rainy day (when drying times are longer). These tiny cracks can be corrected by sanding the wood and repainting with a high-quality paint.

On the other hand, there are stress cracks. These are cracks in the structure beneath the surface that break through and crack the paint. They are typically found at corners but may be anywhere.

Small corner stress cracks are fairly common and occur when the home shifts. Large vertical or horizontal stress cracks in exterior walls, however, are less common and are far more serious, as they may indicate a shifting foundation, structural damage or both. If there are extensive stress cracks in the paint, you may wish to call in a structural engineer to evaluate the problem.

Stress cracks in paint can easily be corrected by sanding, sealing and repainting. However, that repair is cosmetic and does not address the stress that caused the problem, which may require foundation or structural wall, ceiling or floor work.

Metal Siding

Numerous types of metal sidings have been used on homes over the past 40 years. Many of these are steel that has been galvanized or otherwise coated with a rust-resisting product. Sometimes this is tin or cadmium, and sometimes it's a tar emulsion. Usually, these forms of siding must be painted to protect the metal from corrosion.

Troubleshooter's Guide

One of the most common reasons owners put metal siding on an older home is to cover up a bad exterior. The existing walls may be clapboard, shingles or some other surface that is worn and deteriorated. Putting new metal siding on almost instantly turns an old home into a new-looking one.

There's nothing wrong with this practice, as long as the existing walls are dry, have no rot and provide a good surface for adhering the siding. Sometimes, however, the old walls contain extensive wood rot and moisture and do not provide a solid nailing surface. The trouble is, it's very hard to tell that this is the case when you look at the completely installed new siding.

When I'm considering an older home with metal siding, I try to peel back the siding at a spot where I can do it unobtrusively and without causing damage. Often this is at the base, at corners or at joints. Just peeling the siding back a fraction of an inch and checking the wall underneath with a good flashlight can speak volumes. Also, check for siding that's hanging at an awkward angle, loose siding or pieces missing, as this will often indicate a bad base.

Siding improperly installed over a wall needing repairs may have to be removed. In other words, you might have to start from the beginning.

Another product is aluminum siding. Here, the paint itself is frequently bonded to the metal. It is sometimes sold with a warranty that claims the siding never needs painting. (Any time you see the word never, watch out!)

In addition, metallic shingles can be adhered to the walls of a home. Again, these either may be paint bonded or may require painting.

When examining metal siding, look for the following:

- Dents or scratches

- Bare metal

- Poorly joined pieces

- Rusted nail heads

Dents or Scratches   The siding is metal; therefore, it's only natural that when you hit it or bounce something off of it, it will dent or scratch. There's nothing wrong with this, except for the unsightly wound it makes, unless the paint has been torn off. If the paint coat was not bonded (or only a light bonding was used), any damage to the metal may result in paint removal.

Look for telltale signs of rust on steel siding. If you find rust, it must be sanded down and repainted. You may want to replace the entire piece of dented siding, although it may be difficult to match the color (particularly after it has baked in the sun for many years).

Bare Metal   Sometimes the paint may not have adhered properly and simply could have peeled off. Or perhaps the metal underneath has oxidized and forced portions of the paint off. Again, check for rust, blisters and peels. They shouldn't be there, but if they are, be cautious about the entire home. A problem on even just a few pieces of siding may indicate bigger problems over all of the siding.

Poorly Joined Pieces   Don't presume that when the siding was put on, it was done correctly. Or if the siding was installed properly, the building could have shifted since then. Look carefully at corners to see that the pieces meet as they are supposed to. If the pieces don't meet properly, are missing or are broken, it could indicate a foundation or structural problem. Generally speaking, ill-fitting pieces of siding may allow moisture to penetrate and damage the wall beneath.

Corrective measures usually involve removing all pieces of siding that abut the problem and either reapplying them or replacing them with new pieces.

Rusted Nail Heads   Rusted nail heads often point to problems underneath the siding. (Rust also indicates that the nails aren't galvanized or made of aluminum.) I've seen walls where the siding itself looked acceptable, except that you could see each nail head clearly because of the tiny ring of rust around it. Just imagine, if the nail heads are rusting like that on the exterior, what's happening on the interior of the metal siding?

You may want to remove a portion of the siding fastened with rusted nail heads to see what damage, if any, has been done on the inside. There may be rusting as well as wood rot beneath, requiring extensive repairs to the wall. (When removing siding, be careful not to dent or scratch it in the process.)

Brick Walls

Bricks are an extremely durable building material, whether they are cement blocks, cinder blocks or clay bricks. Often they are left in their natural state (without painting), as this is considered attractive. When a veneer of bricks is placed against a wall, the same rules apply as for a structural brick wall.

When troubleshooting a brick wall, ask the following questions:

- Are the bricks properly sealed against moisture?

- Are there any cracked or missing bricks?

- If the bricks are painted, is the paint cracked, chipped or peeling?

Proper Sealing   Bricks can form either a solid wall or a facade. If they are a facade, they should be sealed to prevent water from penetrating to the structural wood wall behind.

Bricks and grout, if intact, will normally be enough to keep out moisture. But check the cement between bricks to see that it is intact (not cracked or falling out), hard (not soft indicating improper pouring) and adhering to the bricks. A few pokes here and there with a screwdriver can reveal a great deal. (Both the bricks and the mortar should be hard and difficult to scratch.) Badly laid bricks or a facade where the mortar has deteriorated for one reason or another may need to be replaced or at least sealed. (Some excellent synthetic sealers on the market can handle small mortar cracks.)

Cracked or Missing Bricks   In a structural wall, cracks or missing bricks can indicate a severe problem. In a facade, they may indicate a separation from the wall behind, which is cause for concern if water has penetrated and caused wood rot. You may need to actually remove the facade to determine the damage—an expensive job usually best left to a professional.

A few cracked or chipped bricks here and there are usually not cause for alarm. However, cracks running through a brick wall or facade or missing bricks may be harbingers of trouble.

Chipped, Peeling or Cracked Paint on Bricks   Sometimes a masonry wall, particularly one that is structural, will be sealed and painted. This is often the case in cold-weather climates, where moisture might enter tiny cracks, expand in cold weather and crack the wall.

Check to be sure that the paint is in good order (see above). Look for the usual signs of trouble—paint that is chipping, peeling or cracking. It may indicate moisture coming through from the other side.

Stucco

Stucco is an excellent product and will protect a home for decades, as long as the stucco remains intact. Unfortunately, however, stucco is subject to cracking if there are problems in the wall, and once cracked, it can allow moisture behind it, leading to wood rot.

When examining stucco walls, look for the following:

- Cracks

- Chipped, peeling or chalky paint

Cracks   Even small cracks can be a problem for stucco, because they allow moisture through to the wall behind. Cracks sometimes occur because a home shifts as its foundation settles. Earthquakes, cracked foundations or slabs, poorly constructed walls and badly applied stucco can also cause cracks. Most frequently, you'll see cracks at the corners of windows or doors. These cracks often run diagonally and indicate settling. While they should be filled and sealed, they do not, of themselves, necessarily indicate a serious problem. Horizontal cracks or long vertical cracks in stucco, particularly where one side of the crack is offset from the other, are a different story and may indicate a broken foundation or stucco that has come loose from the wall behind. Have a structural engineer or an expert in stucco and plaster check it out.

Chipped, Peeling or Chalky Paint   Normally, paint is added into the final coat of stucco. In other words, stucco is not normally painted; the paint is in the material itself.

Troubleshooter's Guide

I once had a plasterer friend who swore that stucco should never be painted. He insisted that all you had to do to make it look new again was to wash it with a high-power hose. If you wanted to change the color, you just restuccoed! I could never tell whether he truly believed this or simply was trying to drum up more business for himself.

As a home gets older, its owners frequently repaint the stucco, and once repainted, it is subject to the same problems as any other painted surface. You can check to see whether the stucco is painted by passing your hand over it. If a chalky residue comes off, chances are the residue is dried-out oil paint. You can also find an unobtrusive spot and scratch a line in the surface with your screwdriver. If it's painted, the true color will immediately be revealed beneath the surface. If the color is in the stucco, it will remain constant the depth of the scratch.

Paint that's chipped or peeling may simply indicate a bad paint job or poor-quality paint (or paint that was applied over wet stucco or a previous wet paint coat and that has blistered). As long as the problems are superficial (no cracks), the only treatment is usually to remove the current bad paint (usually with a high-pressure hose) and repaint.

Interior

Inside the home, a different type of paint is used—one that contains no (or fewer) fungicides. These days, it is almost always latex based, and the biggest problem is usually that over time, it gets dirty.

Troubleshooter's Guide

Be aware of the difference in the cleanliness of paint when looking at a home that's furnished and one that's empty. Any home with furniture often looks as though the paint is new, even though it might be dirty. Once the furniture has been removed, the walls invariably show marks and scratches. That means that you'll need to repaint. This is something that you may want to negotiate with a seller.

Cracks in the paint are another matter. These may indicate problems with the foundation, or they may simply be minor nuisances.

Upon inspecting the inside of a home, look for the following:

- Scratches and marks
- Cracks

Scratches and Marks

As noted earlier, plan to repaint the interior if you want it to be really clean. Especially watch out for crayon and marking pen marks on the walls. Sometimes these cannot be painted over. Rather, they must be sanded, sealed with shellac, then painted—a fairly time-consuming job.

To see just how badly marked a wall really is, pull a couch or chair away from the wall. Often you'll see all sorts of hidden marks.

Troubleshooter's Guide

Don't think you can wash down walls. It's almost impossible. Each time you wash a portion, you make it cleaner than the surrounding wall areas, which now look dirty. In truth, it probably takes four times as long to wash a wall as to paint it, and the results of washing are often less than desirable.

Cracks

Cracks often occur diagonally at door jambs and at window corners. Mostly, these are cosmetic. If they are small and unob-trusive, the cracks often can be filled quickly, patched, sealed and painted.

Larger cracks, particularly cracks coming through an outside wall, may indicate a more serious problem. Often a cracked foun-dation or slab will be reflected inside. While these cracks may be fixed temporarily, they will return until the underlying problem is fixed.

Sometimes cracks are caused by stress on a home. I have a property that's in the mountains and during the winter, it may receive snow loads as heavy as 150 pounds per square foot. This causes the roof to give under the weight. The result is that the sheetrock on the ceiling and on some walls is forced to expand or contract depending on the weather. As a result, the sheetrock cracks. While these cracks can be dealt with cosmetically, it is virtually impossible to remove them permanently. Every time we have a severe winter, they come back.

Troubleshooter's Guide

Sometimes vertical cracks descending from the lower edges of windows indicate a poorly constructed wall. It may be that the studs supporting the header over the windows were never properly nailed together, and as a result, they move in the wall, causing cracks. You may need to drill screws into the studs (the impact of nailing often results in more damage than it cures) to hold them steady before patching the cracks.

Also, when patching cracks, it may be necessary to replaster and then retexture in order to create a good-looking finish. Be aware, however, that some types of texture used in homes are created with a special gun that blows lightweight plaster onto walls. Short of using this gun (which is expensive and extremely messy), it is very difficult to match the patched area with the older texture. Thus, to do a really good job of removing larger cracks in a home, you may need to do extensive replastering—a fairly expensive proposition.

Roof Annoyances and Serious Defects

THE roof is a home's protection against rain and weather. A good roof, therefore, is essential to not only a dry but also an undamaged home. Let the roof deteriorate, and the home will soon follow.

Roof problems usually take the form of leaks. These can be difficult to spot from the outside. In fact, the surface of a roof may look perfectly sealed. However, if you view the roof from the attic, you may quickly spot water marks where it is leaking. If the leaks are severe, you may be able to spot them easily on the home's ceilings as discolorations. Furthermore, the ultimate test of a roof is how well it sheds water. If the owners permit it, spray the roof with a garden hose. While that may not provide enough water to reveal a small leak, it might be enough to show a severe leak.

The big problem with roofs is that they are extremely expensive to replace and repair. Today, replacing a roof in some areas may cost $10,000 to $15,000, depending on the quality of materials used and the cost of labor. Just fixing a few leaks can easily run up into $500 if they are difficult to get to.

All of which is to say, when inspecting a home, pay special attention to the roof.

Checking Out the Roof

We'll get into specific types of roofs and what to look for in a moment, but let's begin with a few guidelines on inspecting the roof. Generally speaking, for a proper inspection, get as close to both the top and the underside of the roof as possible. On top, you may be able to climb a ladder or lean out a second-story window, but be careful. No inspection is worth a fall from a roof! On the surface, you're looking for anything irregular—shingles falling off, curled or broken shingles, a sagging roofline or anything else that suggests something may be wrong. We'll discuss specifics shortly.

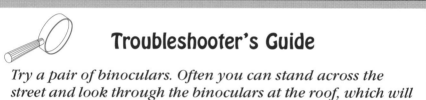

Troubleshooter's Guide

Try a pair of binoculars. Often you can stand across the street and look through the binoculars at the roof, which will be as clear as if you were only a few feet away. You should be able to see the roof's condition and possibly even its problems, while remaining on the ground. It's an old contractor's trick.

You also will want to get under the roof, if possible. Ideally, there's an attic, and you can get inside. Be sure you do this during the day. When you look up at the underside of the roof, you may be surprised. I've examined at roofs that had so much sunlight pouring through that they looked almost like windows! Holes in the roof usually (but not always) leak.

Also, as noted earlier, look for water stains. If there is insulation, look for water stains and puddling on it. Check the framing supporting the roof for cracks and dry rot. Similarly, look at the decking (plywood pieces or long boards) on top of the framing. Pull on the framing to make sure it's secure (but don't pull hard if it's rotten).

Now let's consider problems with specific types of roofs.

Specific Types of Roofs

Wood Shingle Roofs

Wood shingles generally come in three sizes: light (standard), medium and heavy shake. The light shingle has a life span of about 15 years under normal conditions. Medium shake may go 20 to 25 years, and heavy shake, 25 to 35. Of course, these are only guidelines; they could last longer or shorter, depending on the severity of weather in the area.

One problem with wood shingles is that they are flammable. They can be dipped in a flame retardant solution, which helps, but my own experience has been that after a few years on the roof, this retardant no longer functions well. In urban fires in California in 1993 and 1994, wood-shingle-roof homes often burned down, while homes with other types of nonflammable shingles, often right next door, survived. It's something to consider.

When inspecting wood shingle roofs, check for the following problems:

- Shingles falling off on the outside

- Tar paper showing through the shingles

- Holes underneath

- Leaks

Shingles Falling Off Sometimes you can tell the true condition of a roof by searching the ground at the edge of the home. A lot of shingles lying about suggests that the wooden roof may be worn and cracked and that the shingles are falling apart.

Pick up one or two of these shingles, and examine them for burn-throughs. These are tiny holes in the shingles that were once black or dark spots, which have caught the sun's rays and, over the years, actually burned through. Burn-throughs usually occur only on light, thin wood shingles. If they're present on a few, chances are burn-throughs are common to all the shingles and could lead to leaks.

Also, check the size of the fallen shingles. Are they large and complete, suggesting that the nailing is coming loose? Or are they thin, cracked pieces, suggesting that the shingles have dried out and are falling apart?

You can tell a lot from the wood shingles that fall off. Ideally, of course, you will find no fallen shingles on the ground.

Tar Paper Showing Through   Now get close to the roof (either get on it, or use binoculars, as suggested above). (Note: When on a shingle roof, be careful that you don't crack the shingles as you walk on them.) Look for missing shingles. You can usually tell these by following the rows with your eyes. Each row should overlap the next all along the roof. Empty spaces mean shingles are missing.

In the spaces, look to see whether black tar paper shows through. Usually, a shingle roof will have a deck composed of plywood (older homes have roofs constructed of planks of wood), on top of which are placed rows of tar paper. It's the tar paper that finally keeps out the water, although the shingles on top protect it and, if placed correctly, will keep most of the tar paper dry. If the paper shows, it is unprotected, and the sun and wind will soon deteriorate it, allowing water to enter the home. Seeing tar paper where shingles should be is a bad sign.

Holes Underneath   As noted earlier, you'll have to get into the attic to check for holes underneath the roof. Be sure you do it during daylight hours, preferably under sunlight. When in the attic, look up. You should see nothing but darkness.

Troubleshooter's Guide

Just because there are holes doesn't mean the roof will leak. Remember, wood swells when it gets wet. Small holes can close up. Furthermore, when a wood hole is small enough, water not under pressure simply won't go through it. I've seen roofs where there were spaces perhaps a quarter-inch wide and 4 inches long, yet—remarkably—little to no water leaked through. A roof might continue in this condition for several years before it suddenly begins leaking badly.

If you see pinpricks of light everywhere, like stars in a night sky, the wood shingles are probably burned through in many spots, and the damage has gone through the felt paper beneath. (Of course, check to see whether there is felt paper; some roofers skip it. Without felt paper, the roof may not leak when it's new but will probably leak badly after it ages and the shingles begin to deteriorate.) If you see a lot of light, check with a roofer; the entire roof may need to be replaced.

If you see light coming through in only one area, it may mean that wind has damaged the shingles there. Corrective action may require only a patch job rather than a complete replacement.

Leaks As noted earlier, leaks usually appear as stains. You can detect these in the attic, on the ceiling below or sometimes on the walls both inside and outside the home. Leaks indicate a serious problem that requires a remedy, perhaps including patching and repainting discolored ceilings and walls. Consult with a good roofer to see whether the problem can be patched or whether the roof is so old it needs to be replaced.

Asphalt and Fiberglass (Composition) Shingle Roofs

Perhaps the greatest improvements in roofs in recent years have come in the form of asphalt and fiberglass shingles. They have been made more durable and certainly more appealing to look at, and their price has been cut to the point where they are usually the cheapest alternative. A modern inexpensive roof of this type may now be rated for 25 years (which means, in extreme climates, it will probably last at least half that time).

Problems with asphalt and fiberglass shingles are that they tend to dry out, are heavy and add to the load of the roof and, at least in the past, were unattractive. Some of the cheapest ones, in my opinion, are still unattractive.

When troubleshooting an asphalt and fiberglass shingle roof, watch for the following problems:

- Leaking
- Mixed layers of shingles
- Inflexible shingles
- Curling

Leaking   Check underneath the roof and inside the home. Leaks should be apparent, although you probably won't see them from the rooftop. (See also the earlier sections in this chapter on detecting leaks.)

Mixed Layers   Sometimes homes built about 30 years ago had light-wood-shingle roofs that lasted only about 15 years. When it came time to replace, the owner did not remove the worn-out shingles but instead laid down a new roof of inexpensive composition shingles on top of the wood. Perhaps this eventually wore out, and a second and even a third layer of composition shingles was placed on top. In the end, the roof was a sandwich of different types of shingles.

There are several problems with this practice. Probably the most dangerous is weight. Roofs are built for a certain load, which includes the weight of shingles. Each time you add a layer, you increase that weight. (Asphalt shingles are extremely heavy, typically anywhere from 200 to 300 pounds per 100 square feet. Each time you reshingle, you can be adding tons of weight.) Snow adds the threat of roof collapse. A moist climate adds the possibility of moisture build-up between the layers and, therefore, possible deterioration of the wood beneath. Dry country adds the chance that the top layers of shingles will curl or dry out (see "Curling" below). Finally, sometimes the bottom layers will cause the top layers to wear unevenly, giving the roof an awkward if not unattractive appearance.

Inflexible Shingles   When asphalt and fiberglass shingles are new, they will bend a little bit. They won't bend much, but if you pull on an edge, it will curl slightly.

Over time, however, the chemicals that keep the shingles flexible (usually a mineral oil of some sort) can dry out from the heat and radiation of the sun. When this happens, the shingles become inflexible. Pry up a tiny corner of one, and see whether it breaks off in your hand. Rub this piece in your hand to see whether it crumbles into dust. When that happens, the roof is worn out and needs to be replaced.

Curling   In extremely hot climates, particularly in the Southwest, the heat often dries out old shingles to the point where the edges curl up. The roof, or a portion of it, will actually look Oriental in design, curling upward.

When a roof begins to curl, it is a sure sign that it is dried out and will soon need to be replaced. The curled portions may break off, leading to leakage, and the roof may begin to crumble.

Other Types of Shingled Roofs

An increasing variety of shingles are now available on the market, although most of the new shingles are costly and are most likely to be found on expensive homes. Shingle types include slate, concrete, plastic and an asbestos-cement combination.

All of these shingles, with the exception of plastic, tend to be heavy and, when used as replacements on an older home, often require that supports be added to the roof to withstand the weight. You may want to have a competent roofer check out an older home with a new, heavy roof to be sure adequate supports were put in place and that trusses inside are not sagging.

The problems likely to occur with most of these shingled roofs are similar to those of tile roofs (see "Tile Roofs," below).

Tar and Gravel Roofs

Tar and gravel are used primarily on flat surfaces or very low slopes. Tar is laid down with layers of tar paper. Then gravel is sprinkled on top. The gravel protects the tar and paper from damage.

When inspecting a tar and gravel roof, watch for the following:

- Leaks and drainage problems

- Areas of no gravel and shrinkage (at the edges)

- Bubbling, curling and crumbling

Leaks and Drainage Problems   Finding leaks on a flat tar and gravel roof can be difficult because you usually don't have any attic or crawlspace under the roof. That means you can check only the ceiling underneath for water marks and damp areas.

Another concern with this type of roof is puddling. Ideally, when water strikes the roof, it will run off to the sides and eventually to the gutters and downspouts—if the roof is pitched properly. However, some roofs have low spots, where water puddles. This can be caused by poor design or construction or simply by the warping of wood under the roof over time.

You might be able to sight along a roof with your eye to check for low areas, but the only sure way to tell is with a hose. You should be able to see fairly quickly whether and where puddles form.

Another way to check for low areas is to jump up and down on the roof. A solid, well-built roof won't give. A problem roof will spring down and back up, indicating that when water puddles on the top, its weight may push the roof down, causing an even bigger puddle and, possibly, even some structural problems. (Be careful; some roofs are so rotted that you can fall through by jumping.)

No Gravel and Shrinkage   A tar and gravel roof needs gravel on the top; this protects the tar. However, sometimes the gravel will be blown or washed away, exposing the tar. This usually takes the form of a black spot. Tar exposed in this way is vulnerable to cracks, breaks and leaks and may soon need to be replaced or at least retarred and regraveled.

Shrinkage occurs when the sun beats down on the exposed tar and dries it out. Usually, you see this at the edges when the tar is pulled away from flashing. It, too, can result in leaks.

Bubbling, Curling and Crumbling   On a well-laid roof, the tar and gravel will be perfectly flat, indicating that they are adhering to the surface below. In a poor roof job, there may be bubbles, some quite large. The trouble with these bubbles is that they can crack, allowing moisture to get directly at the wood subroof below. Sometimes, however, one tar and gravel roof has been laid over another (when the first wore out), and the bubbles, though cracked, might not leak. If you see bubbles, hire a good contractor to evaluate the problem.

As is true of an asphalt roof, a tar and gravel roof can deteriorate in the hot sun until it literally crumbles, almost into dust. Some curling can likewise occur. If you see curling and are able to break off a small piece, then crumble it in your hand, you could be looking at the need for a new roof.

Tile Roofs

Tile roofs are most frequently found in the Southwest. When properly constructed and maintained, they can last almost indefinitely. In the last century, they were fashioned by very carefully interlacing pieces of tile and using mortar to hold them in place. Modern tile roofs typically have an underlayer of heavy felt that keeps out water, while the tiles themselves keep out most water and all wind and weather.

Troubleshooter's Guide

In several developments in Southern California a few years ago, the roofing contractor failed to put the felt under the tiles, which were laid in summer. When winter rains came, water was forced under the tiles, and the roofs leaked terribly. The real tragedy was that there was no way to fix the problem, short of removing all of the tiles, placing the needed felt paper in place and then retiling. This, of course, was a terribly expensive job. The moral here is that if you're buying a brand-new home with a tile roof that hasn't yet been weather tested, be sure you've got an excellent guarantee from the builder.

When you are examining a tile roof, watch for the following problems:

- Leaks
- Cracked tiles

Leaks   Check for leaks in the attic and on the ceiling in the room below, as well as on inside and outside walls. When a tile roof leaks, it usually pours, so you probably won't have difficulty finding leaks if they exist. You can test the roof by spraying large amounts of water with a hose, but be sure you get the owner's permission first, in case there's a severe leakage problem.

Cracked Tiles Cracked tiles are a real problem with tile roofs. Therefore, never walk on a tile roof. Doing so will often crack the tiles. So will branches blown onto the roof from nearby trees. Look at the roof from a distance using binoculars. Broken tiles suggest that leaks may occur.

Metal Roofs

Metal roofs can be made out of a wide variety of materials, from copper (found on many older commercial buildings) to aluminum and steel. Steel roofs are usually galvanized, but they could be stainless or they could have a tin coating.

As long as metal roofs aren't punctured, torn or allowed to oxidize, they can last indefinitely. They are frequently found in areas where there is snow because they tend to shed it well. On the other hand, older metal roofs tend to expand in the heat of the sun and create cracking and popping sounds, making them quite noisy to live under.

When troubleshooting a metal roof, determine whether the following problems exist:

- Punctures and tears

- Discoloration, peeling paint and rust

Punctures and Tears Punctures typically occur when branches of trees bounce onto metal roofs. The metal is often quite thin, and it may not take much of a blow to puncture it. Tears usually occur when the wind catches a corner of a metal sheet and lifts it up. Sometimes only a small tear will occur. However, if left uncorrected, this could whip up in the next windstorm and tear off huge pieces of the roof. Any puncture or tear can lead to leaking and can result in further damage to the roof. Metal roofs aren't that difficult to fix, but you need a competent roofer, and few specialize in metal.

Discoloration, Peeling Paint and Rust One of the problems with metal roofs is that they can be difficult to paint. Paint simply doesn't adhere to them very well, although special paint preparations stick better to galvanized metal and tin. Aluminum roofs often come anodized, which means that the paint has been electrically adhered to the surface, a process that usually works well for at least ten years, provided the surface isn't damaged. If a metal roof is discolored, don't assume you can simply slap a coat of paint on it. The paint might peel off within one season. You might need to put on a new roof in order to get it to look good again. Check with a roofer who specializes in metal.

Only steel rusts, and rusting often follows punctures and tears. Once metal has begun rusting, it must be repaired promptly, else the rust spot will grow larger. If you have a metal roof and find a corner or edge that is rusting, carefully check the entire roof. The whole thing may be rusting.

Flashing, Gutters and Downspouts

Gutters and downspouts can be wood, metal or plastic. Plastic is usually preferred these days because it is lightweight, will not rust or rot and is easy to install. Flashing is usually metal (galvanized steel or aluminum). It is used in the valleys and other areas of a roof where it is difficult, if not impossible, to get a tight fit with shingles.

It is important to understand the purpose of having gutters and downspouts. (Flashing is obviously necessary to keep roofs from leaking.) Basically, the gutters and downspouts catch rainwater from the roof and lead it away from the home. The idea is to keep the excess rainwater that falls off the roof from getting too close to the foundation, undermining it and seeping under the home. If a home has good drainage away from the foundation due to the natural slope and contours of the land, no gutters and downspouts may be necessary. (Sometimes a simple metal deflector can be placed on the roof to keep rainwater away from entrances.) Don't be alarmed because a home doesn't have gutters or downspouts; it may not need them. On the other hand, if there are indications of standing water under the home or problems with the foundation, have an engineer check out the drainage system.

If a home has gutters, chances are it needs them. Check that they aren't clogged and filled with leaves. This defeats their purpose. Gutters and downspouts need to be cleaned out at least once a year, usually right before the rainy season.

When examining flashing, gutters and downspouts, look for signs of the following:

- Leaks, rust and cracks

- Separation from the home

- Rotting

Leaks, Rust and Cracks   It can be very difficult to tell when roof flashing is leaking because the water may travel long distances along joists. In other words, the leak may appear in a ceiling many feet away from where it's actually coming through the roof.

You have two common ways to detect flashing leaks. If the flashing is visible on the roof surface, examine it for tears, holes and rust. If the flashing appears to have a lot of rust on the visible surface, chances are it may have completely rusted out on the part that's under the shingles. Also, if possible, look at the flashing from underneath, in the attic. Have a friend spray water on it with a hose while you examine it closely. You may be able to see the leak clearly. (Note: Flashing is also used at the eaves of a roof, and leaks there commonly will flow back from the eaves and appear as water pouring down the side of the home.)

Separation   Over time, gutters and downspouts may rust out, rot out (see "Rotting," below) or be damaged by branches falling from trees. When that happens, they will often come loose and separate from the home. This is easily seen by walking around the home and examining them. All gutters and downspouts should look neat and trim against the home. If they are bent, sagging or separated, they need repair work.

Rotting   Older homes often have wood gutters. When new, these function quite well. But over time, water tends to stagnate in them, and they rot—typically, at the very bottom. However, sometimes rotting is difficult to see, particularly if the wood hasn't yet collapsed. Running water from a hose onto the roof and into the gutters will usually reveal the problem—but not always, particularly if the gutters are choked with leaves. Discoloration at the very bottom of a gutter is another giveaway that there's a problem.

Troubleshooter's Guide

This chapter tells you what to look for, but you're probably not an expert and still may not be sure about a roof. If that's the case, call in an expert. Ask a home inspector about a roofer. Get recommendations from brokers, as well as several opinions. There's always a possibility that a roofer may find fault where there is none simply because he needs the work.

Water System Problems

A home has two water systems. The first brings fresh water in; the second takes sewage out. Both are vital to your enjoyment of the home, and if either breaks down, repairs can be costly. That's why it's very important that you have a good sense of the condition of the home's water systems before you buy (and if you're a seller, that you likewise know the condition so that you can prepare for a buyer's possible demands for repairs to a defective system).

This chapter will not dwell much on how a system works. Instead, it will look at quick and easy checks you can do that should bring you up to speed on the water system's condition. Of course, if you inspect the home along with a professional, he or she may have equipment to perform additional tests (such as water pressure gauges), but you'll want to be sure the inspector pays attention to the following tests as well.

Fresh Water Inspection—Interior

Most water usage occurs inside the home (we'll discuss outside bibs, sprinklers and wells later). Therefore, it's important that as you walk through the home, you carefully check for problems in the bathrooms, kitchen and utility room.

Faucets

When inspecting a home's faucets, check for the following:

- Leaks

- Rusting and other pipe problems

- High or low water pressure

Leaks   In the bathrooms, kitchen and utility room, examine the hot and cold water faucets. Look for deposits on the faucets themselves and on the surrounding counter surfaces. Normally, when you turn on the water, it runs only from the spigot, and there's no water at the faucet itself. However, when faucets get old, they tend to leak, often at the stems, and water seeps out around them.

You also might see moisture, which may increase when you turn on the faucet. There may be calcium deposits, a kind of white scale indicating not only leakage, but hardness in the water. There could be a blue-green stain, which would indicate some leaching of copper into the water (to be discussed later).

Normally, if the faucets were produced by major manufacturers (such as Delta, Moen or Price/Pfister), replacement parts may be available, and leaks at the faucet can be repaired quickly at nominal cost, particularly if you do it yourself.

Rusting and Other Pipe Problems   Now turn on the water in the sink. Look carefully at the water that first comes out. If the home is in use, the water will probably appear clear. However, if the home hasn't been occupied for a while, the water may be discolored.

A red, rusty color indicates that the pipes are probably galvanized steel and could be rusting. Galvanized steel pipes often begin rusting heavily after about 15 years of usage and, depending on how quickly they rust, may need to be replaced. If you notice reddish water, check the pipes carefully in the attic and basement, as indicated later in this chapter.

Bluish water suggests copper in the pipes. This is an uncommon condition, but when it occurs, it can be serious. Check with your local water supplier for further information and possible remedies. (Sometimes inadequate chlorination may cause leaching of copper from copper pipes into the water system.)

Now flush the toilet. After it refills, look in the bottom of the bowl for any tiny metallic particles. These often show up as shiny grit-like reflections. If the home has galvanized steel pipes, these particles may indicate that rust and corrosion exists in the cold water side.

Next, stop the sink, turn on the hot water and let the bowl half fill; then turn off the water, let it settle and examine the bowl. If you notice these same particles, it could mean that there is also corrosion in the hot water heater that is getting through the pipes. Check the age and condition of the hot water heater.

Now unplug the drain, and lean under the sink to feel the S-shaped pipe, called the trap. If it is moist, the drainage pipe under the sink (plastic or thin metal) may be either leaking or corroded. Oftentimes the pipe will leak because it was never properly installed, the attaching pipe being either too long or too short. Plastic pipe almost never corrodes, but metal pipe does frequently. Feel the very bottom of the trap, and press in gently with your finger. If the metal is soft or squishy, it is ready to fail and will have to be replaced. Fortunately, replacement is inexpensive—again, especially if you do it yourself.

Finally, turn on the water in the sink and tub/shower. After it has been on awhile, turn off the faucets. Give them a snug turn, but don't force them. Does the water stop running? It should. If it doesn't, the washer is probably bad and may need to be replaced. Again, with a major faucet manufacturer, this shouldn't be a problem. Keep in mind, however, that it's much harder to change the washer in a tub/shower. (Also, the water may continue to drip from a shower head or tub spigot for a minute or more after it has been shut off until the lines clear. There's nothing abnormal about this, as long as the water eventually does stop.) Sometimes the problem is more than just the washer. The "seat" that washer seals against may itself be pitted. Seat grinders are available; however, in severe cases, the entire faucet may have to be replaced.

High or Low Water Pressure   You want enough water pressure in the home so that if all of the faucets are turned on, the toilet is flushed and someone is taking a shower, there's enough water to go around. Having enough water pressure is a function of three things: the pressure of water coming into the home, the size of the pipe leading to the faucets, toilet and so forth and the condition of that pipe.

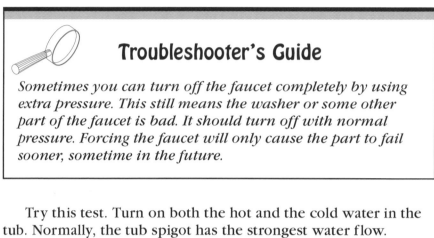

Troubleshooter's Guide

Sometimes you can turn off the faucet completely by using extra pressure. This still means the washer or some other part of the faucet is bad. It should turn off with normal pressure. Forcing the faucet will only cause the part to fail sooner, sometime in the future.

Try this test. Turn on both the hot and the cold water in the tub. Normally, the tub spigot has the strongest water flow. Indeed, the water should pour into the tub. Now turn on both the hot and the cold faucets in the sink, and watch the flow in the tub. It should not be greatly diminished. Finally, flush the toilet. Again, the flows into the tub and the sink should not be greatly affected.

Troubleshooter's Guide

You can have your water utility or city check water pressure at the meter, or you can buy a small water pressure gauge and check it yourself. With galvanized pipe, if the pressure is low and the water is rusty and particles come out, you can feel fairly confident that the pipe is partially blocked due to corrosion or build-up of deposits. This is a serious problem because the home may have to be replumbed. Check into the section on pipes, below.

If the flows are significantly reduced, there probably is a water pressure problem. The most likely culprit is corrosion within the pipes (normally, this happens only to galvanized steel) or insufficient water pressure in the home.

Another problem you may face is unequal flow on the hot and cold sides. This is noticed most dramatically when someone takes a shower and someone else flushes a toilet. The sudden drop in water pressure on the cold side (toilets use only cold water) may make the water temperature of the shower shoot up. This is not only inconvenient, it could be dangerous.

To test for this, run the shower until there is adequate hot water, then create a warm mixture. Now flush the toilet, preferably in an adjoining bathroom. Does the water temperature suddenly become very hot? If so, the pipes have been plumbed incorrectly, perhaps with the wrong size pipe leading to the toilet or shower. Correction here could be very expensive, requiring replumbing of part of the home.

Toilets

When troubleshooting a home's toilets, watch for the following problems:

- Bad mechanisms

- Leaks

- Poor drainage

Bad Mechanisms   Each toilet is connected to both the fresh water coming into the home and the sewage system going out. Therefore, you can check both systems here at the same time.

Troubleshooter's Guide

If the lid of the toilet is missing or broken, you'll probably have to replace the entire toilet. It's almost impossible to find a matching lid, and if you do, it will probably cost as much as a new toilet. Similarly, if the toilet or the tank is cracked, it will have to be replaced for the same reason.

Leaks   Lift the lid of the toilet, and flush it. The water should drain quickly from the storage tank; then the toilet should begin filling immediately. If water sprays out at you or if there's a loud groaning noise, the inside mechanism may have to be replaced. Again, it's inexpensive if you do it yourself.

The water level should rise in the bowl; then the inflow should stop. If water keeps coming in, even at a very slow rate, it probably means that the stopper at the bottom of the storage tank is defective and may need to be replaced. These days, new seats with stoppers can be purchased for less than $10 at most hardware stores. (You will want to fix this because even a slow leak can waste an enormous amount of water over a month's time.)

Troubleshooter's Guide

You can often determine the true age of a home by turning over the toilet lid and examining the inside surface. Often the date of manufacture is stamped there. If they're the original toilet and lid, they probably were installed very close to that date, at the time the home was built.

A more serious leak can occur at the base of the toilet, where it joins the plumbing in the home. Basically, the toilet is connected by means of a wax seal. If properly fitted, this seal will last the lifetime of the toilet and the home. However, it can be damaged in a variety of ways. For example, sometimes children drop small toys down the toilet, and these get stuck in the trap below the toilet seat. To remove them, an owner may lift up the toilet (it's normally held in place with only two bolts) and set it back down. Unless the wax seal is replaced, however, it may no longer be seated correctly, and when the toilet flushes, it may allow water to seep out onto the floor.

Another rarer problem can occur if, at some time, hot water is poured down a toilet. I once knew a family who made beer in their bathroom and, for a time, let hot water flow into the toilet.

This melted the seal to the point where it leaked and had to be replaced.

To check for this problem, flush the toilet several times, then look closely at where the toilet edge meets the floor. The surface should be dry and dusty to the touch. Any moisture indicates a leak. Reseating the toilet with a new seal should correct the problem.

This test is very difficult if there's carpeting in the bathroom and a tiny leak. Sometimes, however, odor near the base of the toilet suggests the presence of a leak under the carpeting that you can't see. You may want to get permission from the homeowner to pull back the carpeting an inch or so to inspect the surrounding floor.

Poor Drainage   Finally, be sure the toilet drains properly. To check this, flush the toilet, and watch how the water goes down. In a normal flush, a vortex forms quickly, and the water flushes out forcefully. In a problem toilet, the vortex may be shallow and weak, and the water may never fully flush.

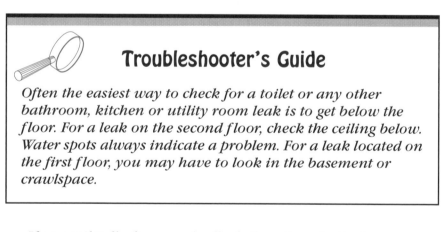

Troubleshooter's Guide

Often the easiest way to check for a toilet or any other bathroom, kitchen or utility room leak is to get below the floor. For a leak on the second floor, check the ceiling below. Water spots always indicate a problem. For a leak located on the first floor, you may have to look in the basement or crawlspace.

If one toilet flushes poorly, flush the others in the home, assuming it has more than one bathroom. If the other toilets flush normally, it's probably something stuck in the problem toilet's trap. As noted earlier, this requires removing the toilet and checking from the bottom. Be sure to use a new wax seal when replacing it. Unless you're very handy, this is something you'll want a plumber to do.

If all toilets flush slowly, you may have a far more serious problem with drainage from the home. Check the section that discusses sewage problems.

Garbage Disposal

When you examine a garbage disposal, check for the following:

- Improper operation

- Leaks

Improper Operation   Disposals can last as long as ten years but not usually much longer. If the disposal operates properly, it will chew up almost anything you throw down it, and it will do this quietly and with a minimum of vibration. *Note: At no time should you put your hand down the garbage disposal while it is connected to a live electrical circuit.*

Without turning on the water, run on the garbage disposal for a moment. It should turn on instantly and hum quietly. Any loud banging noises may indicate a broken mechanism. (Note: Some inexpensive garbage disposals tend to make a lot of noise during normal operation.) Feel the sink while the disposal is working. There should be little to no vibration. If there is a large vibration, the disposal may be improperly attached. If you don't know how to attach it yourself, have a plumber check it out.

Troubleshooter's Guide

Look under the sink to see the horsepower rating of the disposal. One-third horsepower normally is minimal. It will work but will tend to get stuck frequently. One-half horsepower or more is better. These will chew up almost

---

Leaks   Look at the overall condition of the disposal. If it is covered with rust stains, it is probably leaking. The leak may be coming from the pipe connection leading out or from the sink due to improper attachment. After running the disposal with water and with the disposal off, feel under the sink near the disposal. Is it wet? If so, water may be leaking where the disposal is attached. If it's dry, feel the pipe that drains water from the dishwasher into the disposal. Is this wet? If so, that could be the problem. (Note: It is always possible that both the attachment and the drain are leaking.)

If everything feels dry so far, feel the bottom of the disposal. If it is wet, the problem is probably that the disposal is leaking and should be replaced.

A new disposal can be purchased for much less than $100, but it can be difficult to install. I know. I've put in many of them, and unless you're very handy, I suggest the services of a plumber.

Dishwasher

Most homes these days offer a dishwasher. If the unit is more than three years old, it will probably look pretty beat up. After about five to seven years of constant use, it may need to be replaced. A new dishwasher costs anywhere from less than $300 on up, depending on features and quality.

When checking a dishwasher, watch for the following problems:

- Poor operation (including leaks)

- Rusting

- Overflow obstruction

Poor Operation   Dishwashers all have timers. Turn on the dishwasher when you first begin your home inspection, and let it run through its full cycle. This will take a half an hour or more, during which time you can check out other features of the home.

If the dishwasher does not complete its cycle, check to see that its door is completely closed and that the unit is plugged in. (It usually plugs into a wall socket located under the sink.) If the dishwasher still doesn't work, the timer may be bad. If it is the timer, expect to pay $100 or more to have it replaced. This is a job for an appliance professional.

If the dishwasher completes its cycle, open the door and look to see whether there's water left inside. A little is normal, but an inch or more indicates improper draining. Either the pump may be bad or the drain clogged.

Rusting   Dishwashers incorporate a lot of steel, and even though it has been porcelainized, painted or rubber coated, eventually the steel will begin to rust. Check for rusted-through shelves inside. Often these can be replaced at a nominal cost. Also check for rust just inside at the bottom of the door, either on the door itself or on the pan. This is the area that tends to rust first. Poke at the rust with your screwdriver. If it's just on the surface, the rusting probably won't be a problem for several years. However, if the area has been rusting for some time, the metal may break away; indeed, the splash plate on the door or even the top of the inside pan may be rusted away. This could lead to water leaking out of the dishwasher. At this stage, it's usually cheaper and easier to replace the appliance than to try to repair it.

Overflow Obstructions   Finally, check the overflow valve. Most localities require this in their building codes. It should be located on top of the counter near the sink (or actually coming through an opening at the top of the sink). The overflow valve regulates water coming out of the dishwasher and flowing into the plumbing, usually into the garbage disposal.

Run the dishwasher until it fills, then move the timer until it begins to drain. Now watch the overflow. No water should come out. If water does overflow, the drain is plugged. Usually, this can be cleared fairly easily, but it may take a plumber to do it if you're not handy.

Tubs and Showers

Things to check out:

- Leaks

- Scratches and cracks

We've already discussed water inflow problems on tubs and showers under the "Faucets" section. However, some other problems are possible with these units that should be covered separately.

Leaks   Tubs normally don't leak since they are sealed units. However, they can develop leaks in three areas: the drain at the bottom, the overflow in the front wall and the top edge. Leaks in the drain and overflow normally will not be apparent in the bathroom unless you find some water seeping out onto the floor from under the tub. A better place to check is the ceiling below (if it's a two-story home) or under the floor (from the crawlspace or basement). Water leaks from the tub will be most apparent there as wetness or stains.

Water leaking over the edge may occur if a sliding glass door has been installed on the wall of a tub and shower combination. When the shower is turned on, water may splash the door, and if its seals are broken or if the drains to the inside of the tub are clogged, water may leak out onto the floor. Similar leakage may occur when a shower curtain is placed improperly.

Check for proper aiming of the shower head and for water damage on the wall and floor near the leak. Dry rot could have set in, which may require that a portion of the wall and floor be replaced.

Note: Do not attempt the following check unless you first receive written approval from the owner, as it may cause damage to walls, ceilings or furniture if the shower is defective.

To check a *shower* for leaks, the usual procedure is to plug the drain with a cloth or vinyl plug, then turn on the shower. The water level will rise until it's close to overflowing. Ideally, there will be no leaks out the sides of the shower or from below. However, if the pan (usually a galvanized metal box, although in older homes, it could be made from wood that has been tarred) is defective, water will leak out. In this case, the pan must be replaced, along with any wood that shows signs of dry rot— usually a costly procedure involving removing the floor of the shower and putting in a new floor (and pan). Any tile work in the shower also will have to be replaced.

Scratches and Cracks   Scratches and cracks on sink countertops, inside stall showers and elsewhere in the bathroom are usually considered cosmetic. However, if water is present, be suspicious of dry rot beneath the cracks. Often small, thin-looking cracks can hide big problems.

There is no sure way of checking a crack, short of removing the surface material to see beneath. However, you can gently poke the tile or grout around the crack to determine if it's loose or if it's ready to come up. Push gently. The grout should be equally resistant in all areas. However, if some areas are squishy or tiles seem to go in and out, particularly near a crack, it may indicate that water has gotten beneath the surface and is lifting up the tiles. This may require removal of the surface and replacement of the subsurface. (Note: The true way to check for water beneath scratches and cracks is to poke at their surface with a screwdriver; however, this could cause loose tiles or other materials to pop up, and the homeowner probably would not be happy about this.)

Troubleshooter's Guide

Checking the shower pan is standard procedure for termite inspectors, who also look for dry rot. Some states, such as California, however, may allow inspectors to refuse to check second-floor shower pans for leaking. If the pan is really bad, filling it with water can cause severe leaking and damage to the ceiling underneath, as well as surrounding walls and floors. This can result in an angry owner and a possible lawsuit. It's something to consider before you fill a shower with water.

Water Heater

Storage water heaters use electricity, gas, oil or coal to heat water and store it until you want to use it. Most last anywhere from 7 to 15 years, but all eventually give out, usually when they start to leak. Then the heater must be replaced. A replacement heater can cost anywhere from $200 to $400 or more. When checking the heater, look for several safety features, as well as at the condition of the heater itself.

When you investigate a water heater, check for the following things:

- Old age and insufficient size

- Leaks

- Deposits

- Inoperative safety pressure valve

- Unsafe venting

- Inadequate tie-down

Age and Size   Unless it happens to be stamped on the heater itself, you probably won't know the unit's age, although you may be able to guess by its general appearance. (Don't be fooled, however, by a heater that looks brand new. If it is in a clean location, the heater can go years without getting dirty. On the other hand, a heater with water stains suggests age and use.) Sometimes the homeowner can supply a purchase record. If you don't know the age of the heater, assume it's old and may go out at any time, until you have evidence otherwise.

The size of the heater is also critical. The rule of thumb is that you need ten gallons of water per bedroom, with a 30-gallon minimum. A home with four bedrooms, therefore, needs 40 gallons; a home with five bedrooms, 50 gallons.

If the water heater is too small, you will run out of hot water during a second shower or when washing dishes. (Note: When buying a heater, the difference in cost between a 30-gallon and a 40-gallon heater is usually minimal.)

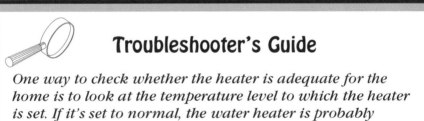

Troubleshooter's Guide

One way to check whether the heater is adequate for the home is to look at the temperature level to which the heater is set. If it's set to normal, the water heater is probably sufficient. If, however, the owner has boosted it to hot, the heater's capacity might be insufficient, and to compensate for this, the temperature has been raised. (With a higher temperature, it takes less hot water and more cold to create a warm mixture.) The trouble with this practice is that at the highest temperature, the wear on the water heater is greater; also, someone could be scalded accidentally.

Another way to check the water heater is to ask to see fuel bills, particularly in the spring and fall, when neither the furnace nor the air conditioner is likely to be on. These bills should reveal what it costs to operate the water heater (usually a substantial portion of the fuel bill). High fuel bills may indicate a heater with too low a capacity.

Leaks   A water heater that leaks is one that must be replaced soon. To check for leaks, look under and at the bottom of the heater. Is water present? Is the bottom of the heater rusted? (Note: If water or rust is present, be sure it is not coming from another source, such as the pipes leading into the heater.)

For all combustion water heaters (all heaters except electric), turn the heater off (you can leave the pilot on), and carefully open the combustion chamber. Now look inside at the metal floor. Is it wet and rusted? Is water dripping from the bottom of the heater onto it? If so, the heater isn't long for this world. (Note: When you first turn on a cold water heater, there will often be condensation on the inside, and water may drip. Don't be alarmed by this because it's perfectly normal. Wait until the heater is fully warmed before checking inside for leaks.)

Deposits   In many areas water contains mineral deposits that build up in the bottom (usually) of combustion heaters. (Rust and corrosion can add to this problem.) As the deposits build, they reduce the efficiency of the heater, as the heat from the bottom element must travel through more material to reach the water. Also, the deposits reduce capacity.

To check for deposits, open the drain valve on the heater slowly until water begins to come out. (If the heater is located in the home, put a pan underneath to catch the water.) The water drains from the bottom of the heater, and any deposits usually will pour out with the water. Water flow that is restricted, even with the valve wide open, suggests that the deposits have accumulated to a level above the valve and are plugging it—not a good sign.

Inoperative Safety Pressure Valve   The building codes in all areas require that each heater be equipped with a temperature and safety pressure valve. In the event that the temperature inside the water heater rises beyond a safe point (as could happen if the automatic temperature control mechanism fails), pressure will build, and this valve will open automatically to release it.

Because extremely hot water or steam could come out of this valve at any time, it should be vented by metal pipes to a safe area outside of the home.

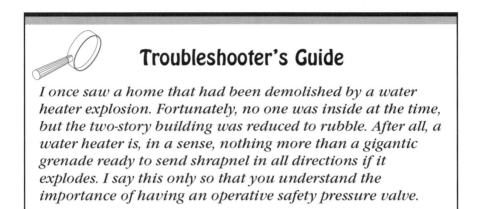

Troubleshooter's Guide

I once saw a home that had been demolished by a water heater explosion. Fortunately, no one was inside at the time, but the two-story building was reduced to rubble. After all, a water heater is, in a sense, nothing more than a gigantic grenade ready to send shrapnel in all directions if it explodes. I say this only so that you understand the importance of having an operative safety pressure valve.

You can check the valve by lifting up on the handle. It should discharge some water, indicating it isn't plugged. Be sure to put the handle back in its former position to close the valve. (Note: Sometimes an old heater and safety valve will contain corrosion and deposits. Yes, the valve may open, but it may not completely close when you push the lever back down. The safety valve could continue to leak indefinitely. Unfortunately, the only cure for this may be to replace the valve.)

Don't confuse the cold water turn-off valve with the safety pressure valve (see Figure 7.1). The turn-off valve is located in line with the cold water pipes. (It's important to have a cold water turn-off valve in the event you need to isolate the hot water heater from the rest of the water supply, as when you're replacing it.)

Also, if two kinds of metal pipe—galvanized and copper—meet at the water heater, be sure that there's a dialectic union between them. (This is a special plumber's union that isolates one metal from the other to prevent electrostatic corrosion.)

While we're on the subject of safety, check to see that any water heater located in a garage, except an electric heater, is at least 18 inches off the floor. Gas fumes from a car are heavier than air, and if you park your car in the garage and it leaks gas, those fumes could reach the water heater's combustion chamber and cause an explosion. However, if the heater is off the ground, it's less likely the fumes will get to the flame.

Unsafe Venting   For all but electric water heaters, there must be a safe vent for exhaust gases. Check the appearance of the vent. All joints should meet, and the vent itself should look sturdy. If a vent leaks or fails, exhaust gases can be emitted directly into the garage or the home and could be deadly. If you're not sure about the vent, ask a plumber.

Inadequate Tie-Down   In earthquake areas, be sure that the water heater is tied to the wall so it won't tip over, causing water leaks and, worse, gas fires.

The tie-down should be heavy metal strapping or chain and should be at or very near the top of the tank. Be sure that the tie-down is fastened securely to surrounding studs in walls with heavy bolts.

Attic and Basement Inspection

No home inspection is complete without checking both the attic and the basement (or the crawlspace under the home, if it has one). This is like lifting the hood of the car to check the engine. When you make your inspection, know what to look for. Be sure to wear clothing that can get dirty, and be careful about climbing into an attic filled with insulation. You might need protective outerwear, as well as a special air filtration mask. Therefore, it could be a job for an expert.

In terms of plumbing, check for the following:

- Leaks

- Pipe problems

- Vent problems

Leaks   You probably won't find a pipe leak in the attic (although if water pipes are routed through there, you could indeed find one). While you're in the attic, however, check the inside of the roof for water marks, suggesting leakage, or light streaming through, suggesting holes that could leak.

In the basement or under the home is where leaks frequently materialize. However, don't examine just the pipes. Find the bathrooms, kitchen and utility rooms located on the floor above, and look beneath them. Many leaks will show up clearly here.

Figure 7.1 Water Heater Showing Safety Pressure Valve, Cold Water Turn-off and Vent

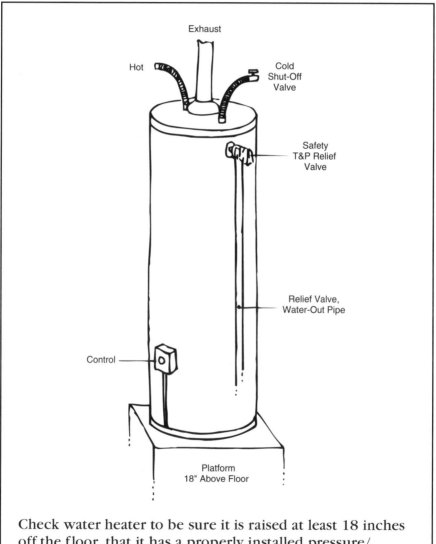

Check water heater to be sure it is raised at least 18 inches off the floor, that it has a properly installed pressure/ temperature relief valve, a cold water shut-off and that the flue is properly vented (for gas heaters).

Pipe Problems   Check to see what kind of pipes are in the home. You can do this at any spot where pipes come out of the walls, such as at the water heater or under a sink between the valve and the wall.

Troubleshooter's Guide

When looking at galvanized steel pipes in an older home, look for compression patches. Frequently, the pipe will rust out and begin to leak. Instead of cutting out the rusted section and replacing it, the homeowner may have bought a compression fitting, which is two pieces of metal with rubber seals and screws. The fitting is placed over the leak and screwed down until the leak stops.

The reason for using these fittings is that if there's one leak in a galvanized pipe, frequently the entire pipe is rusted, and attempting to cut and retread will only result in having the pipe fall apart.

A compression fitting on a galvanized pipe is almost a sure sign that the pipes in the home are rusting out and the entire fresh water plumbing system will soon have to be replaced—a very expensive proposition.

Copper pipes look copper, and galvanized pipes look silver, like steel. If you're not sure, carefully scrape a bit on the pipe's side, and the color should pop right out. There is always the chance that you could have plastic (PVC) pipe in your home, but most localities have not yet approved it for in-home potable water usage.

Copper pipes last almost indefinitely, without problems of corrosion. However, until about five years ago, the fittings were sweated on, using a lead-based solder. Water in the pipes would leach out some of the lead, and this lead would enter into the drinking water.

It's a problem you should be aware of but, in my opinion, not alarmed about. For one thing, this leaching usually stops after about five years. For another, the lead accumulates mostly in standing water, so if you run the tap for a minute or so before using the water, most of the lead will have washed away.

Within the last five years, almost all localities have switched to a type of solder that is lead-free. Hence, the problem today is diminishing.

Galvanized pipes, on the other hand, can be cause for strong concern. Electrolysis, as well as rust and deposits, can clog these pipes and rust them through. (You should have already tested for clogging by looking for reduced water flow in the kitchen sink.)

In addition, look for areas of galvanized pipe that are red with rust or from which water is dripping. Pay careful attention to joints, as these are frequently where rusting is the worst.

Vent Problems   Plastic pipes (usually black), particularly in the attic, are probably sewage vents. Vents prevent water from siphoning out of the traps beneath sinks, tubs and toilets. (The traps fill with water and prevent sewer gases from entering the home.)

Check that these vent pipes are all properly secured and connected. Sewer-like odors in the attic, the basement or any part of the home may indicate that one of these vents has broken or come apart or was never properly installed. It usually will take a plumber to correct the situation.

There may also be metal vents for the furnace, water heater and kitchen stove. For hot vents (from the furnace or water heater), be sure that the insulation is cleared away and that there are no any combustibles near the vents.

Fresh Water Inspection—Exterior

The remainder of your fresh water usage occurs outside the home. Therefore, check carefully the property's outdoor bibs, sprinklers and well, if any.

Hose Bibs and Sprinklers

Hose bibs should be at least 2 feet above ground level and, of course, should not leak (see the section on faucets for a discussion of leakage). Be careful of bibs that are low to the ground (perhaps installed by the homeowner) because polluted water might enter them, then siphon back into the fresh water system. This could poison the system, as well as you and your family.

Sprinklers can be arranged in a wide variety of configurations. In general, they should be placed close enough together to cover the intended watering area (turn them on to see), and their heads should not be broken. Usually, sprinklers are very inexpensive to fix, and you probably can do it yourself.

More important are antisiphon valves. These *must* be on *all* sprinkler lines, and they *must* be located higher than the highest sprinkler head. The danger here (as with low bibs) is that water polluted from the ground might siphon back into the fresh water system of the home, poisoning it. (When the water in a system is shut off, a siphon effect can occur.)

Also, determine whether the sprinklers leak, or even operate. Broken or leaking antisiphon valves should be replaced.

Wells

Although most homes are connected to community water systems, a property may have a private well. Your concerns might run the gamut, from water supply to pump condition to water quality.

A discussion of how to check a private well system is beyond the scope of this book. If you must inspect a well, I strongly urge you to get a contractor who specializes in wells to examine it. Also, obtain certification from the state or at least a private lab concerning the water purity.

Sewage System

The other home water system removes waste water. We've already touched on this in various sections, such as "Toilets" and "Poor Drainage." However, now we'll look at it more directly, in terms of pipe condition, septic tanks and cesspools.

Pipe Condition

The condition of sewer pipes is important because fixing them is expensive. A few years ago, tree roots in the front yard of my home burrowed into the sewer pipe and plugged it. I had to have a plumber excavate and replace about 4 feet of pipe. The cost was $1,200.

The trouble is you can't examine the pipes easily because they are either under the home or buried underground. Therefore, you must check them indirectly.

I suggest you turn on all the faucets in the home (tubs, showers, sinks), then flush all the toilets repeatedly. As you flush the toilets, the water in all of them should vortex down swiftly and completely. If, after a few minutes of this treatment, the toilet flows become sluggish or water backs up in the drains, you probably have detected a problem in the main sewer line. And if the property has a lot of trees, the problem is probably roots.

(Note: Just because water flows freely does not guarantee there is no problem. The owner may have recently had the sewer pipes rooted out by a plumber. This is where full disclosure comes into the act. If you're the buyer, ask the owner whether he or she has ever had the pipes cleared and how long ago. If the owner denies having done so and it later can be determined that he or she did, the owner may have to pay for subsequent repairs. Proving it, of course, is the rub.)

Troubleshooter's Guide

A seller faced with a plugged sewer may offer to call a plumber to root it out for a buyer. This usually costs less than $100. The trouble is that it's rarely permanent. The buyer may have to have it done every few months until, ultimately, the pipe clogs beyond clearing. A better idea would be to have a competent plumber determine a more exact cause and the cost of pipe replacement.

In addition, check around the front and back of the home to determine where the "cleanout" is. This is a pipe coming out of the ground or out of the wall of the exterior of the home with a plug on it. It allows you to open the sewer line, insert a "snake" and clean it out. Some homes are built without cleanouts, even though they are required by codes in most localities. Without a cleanout, a plumber would have to climb onto the roof and snake through a vent to clean it out, a more difficult and costly job.

Septic Tanks and Cesspools

Some localities do not have a public sewer system so instead you must use a septic tank or, less frequently, a cesspool. A septic tank is a highly efficient method of handling sewage waste, but it must be serviced every four or five years. A cesspool is less effective, although servicing prolongs its life somewhat.

A septic tank has two elements: a holding tank, which stores solid waste that can be broken down by bacteria, and a leach field, a wide area of ground criss-crossed with pipes permeated with holes that disperses liquid waste. If the holding tank and leach field are large enough and the soil is sufficiently absorbent, a septic tank can handle the sewage from almost any type of home. However, in moist soil, such tanks are less effective.

The difficulty with septic tanks is that people frequently forget that the holding tank must be pumped out, as noted, about every five years. If it is not pumped out, solid waste will drift into the pipes and into the leach field and plug it. Once plugged, the leach field can never be used again, and to rejuvenate the tank, a new field must be dug. The problem here is finding room on the property for a new field and paying the price (currently $2,500 and up) of installation. A clue that a leach field is failing is wetness on the ground over the field, as well as odor.

Cesspools are less effective than septic tanks. They usually consist of a large hole lined with bricks with layers of permeable clay or soil between the bricks. The idea is that the solid wastes will fill the pool, while the liquids will disperse into the surrounding ground.

Unfortunately, the ground around the tank often gets saturated quickly, and as the solid wastes rise in the pool, they tend to plug the permeable filling between the bricks. Cesspools are seldom used today, but if you discover a property that has one, inspect the cesspool closely. Again, moisture and odor around the cesspool suggest a problem.

Because of the cost involved and the potential health hazards, I suggest you get expert advice on both septic tanks and cesspools. These are not areas in which a beginner should dabble.

Electrical Considerations

IN a modern home, having a working electrical system is absolutely essential. You want to have enough power to operate all your appliances plus any tools you have plus your lights, all at the same time. Furthermore, you want to be assured that you aren't going to get a shock—or worse—from your wall plugs or light fixtures.

Caution

This chapter will examine some ways you can check out a home's electrical system. However, most of these tests involve working with the power on. That means that if there's a problem with the home's electrical system, or if you do something incorrectly, you could be shocked or electrocuted. If you're familiar with home electrical systems, you'll probably not worry much about doing something wrong. On the other hand, if you're new to electrical systems or are concerned about them, simply read this chapter, then ask a professional home inspector to perform the tests for you. Never take chances with electricity. If you don't know what you're doing, get someone who does to do it for you!

Tools

Basically, the only special tool that you will need is a small tester light. These are sold in hardware stores for less than $10. The light comes with two test prongs. When you place each prong in an active circuit, the tester light goes on. If the circuit is dead, it stays off. Be sure to get a tester light that handles from 110 to 220 volts.

Electric Service

Modern homes typically have 200-amp service, at least at the circuit breaker box or fuse box (described below). In addition, they usually have 220 volts in critical areas, such as in the kitchen, so you can hook up an electric stove, and in the washroom, so you can install an electric clothes dryer. If there is no 220-volt service in the home, it is considered a drawback and a reason the price might be lowered. To install 220 volts can cost anywhere from a few hundred to several thousand dollars, depending on whether there is already 220 volts at the box and how close the main box is to the location where you want the power.

Ground Wires

The biggest electrical safety feature in a home is the ground wire. This is the third wire, or the green wire, which should service all of the electrical outlets and should also ground all of the light fixtures.

All plugs and fixtures have at least two wires: the current going out (normally identified as a black wire) from a fuse box or circuit breaker box and the current coming back (normally identified as a white wire). The green wire provides a ground in case of problems. In a wall outlet, typically the black, or "Hot," wire is located on the right side. The white, or "Neutral," wire is on the left, with a slightly larger opening (so a plug can't be inserted backwards). The green, or ground, wire is a round hole in the center bottom. When inspecting the ground wire, check that it operates properly.

Troubleshooter's Guide

Virtually any home built in the last 15 or 20 years should have fully grounded receptacles throughout. However, homes built more than 20 years ago may have only two wires and no ground. While this will supply electricity just as well, in the event of a short caused by a faulty fixture or appliance, it's more likely that someone could get a shock. Unfortunately, the only remedy is to rewire the home, a very, very expensive proposition.

Operation

It's quite easy to test the ground wire for operation (see Figure 8.1). Simply take your tester light and–*being careful to hold the test prongs by the insulation*–stick one end into the Hot opening of a receptacle (usually the right side) and the other end into the Neutral opening (usually the left side). If the circuit is functional, the light will come on.

Now, leaving one test prong in the Hot opening, put the other in the ground opening (the round one at the bottom). Again, the tester light should go on. If the tester light fails to go on, the ground is not operational.

A further check can be done, but this requires that you *turn off the power at the fuse or circuit breaker box.* With the power off, unscrew the face plate of the receptacle, then the two screws holding the receptacle to its box. It should then pull straight out. Check to see that a black wire goes to the right side (Hot) and a white wire goes to the left (Neutral). There should also be either a naked (no insulation) or a green (insulated) ground wire attached directly to the back of the receptacle with a screw (also usually green). Sometimes, if no screw is present, the ground wire is wrapped around the screw that holds the receptacle plug to the wall box.

If the ground wire is missing totally, that receptacle is not wired for a ground (even though the plug itself may have three openings).

Figure 8.1 Plug and Tester Showing Test for Active Ground

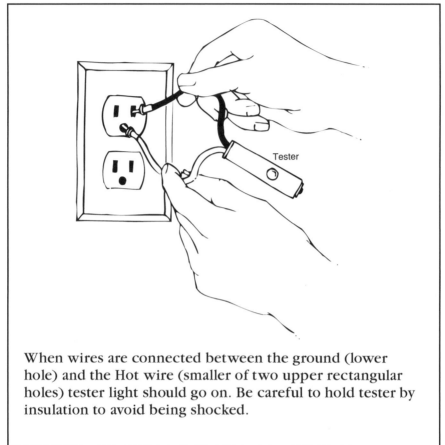

When wires are connected between the ground (lower hole) and the Hot wire (smaller of two upper rectangular holes) tester light should go on. Be careful to hold tester by insulation to avoid being shocked.

Ground Fault Interrupter (GFI) Circuits

All of the circuits in a home lead back to a fuse box or circuit breaker box. In the event of a short at one of the outlets or elsewhere, the fuse will blow or the circuit breaker will trip. The problem is that in some circumstances—for example, a running hair dryer falls into a sink full of water—there could be a delay before the fuse blows or circuit trips and, if you're in contact with the appliance or the water, you could receive a severe, even fatal, shock.

To help avoid this, ground fault interrupter (GFI) circuit breakers should be installed on all outlets in bathrooms, kitchens and utility rooms and outdoors. (Current codes in some communities do not go this far.) A GFI breaker can determine whether there's any leakage to ground (indicating a short) and almost instantly trip the circuit, thus saving you or someone you love from shock or electrocution. The breaker itself is easily distinguished because of its two buttons—one usually marked "Test"; the other, "Reset." "Slave" receptacles can be linked to the GFI breaker, but these can be recognized only by aid of a test (described below).

Troubleshooter's Guide

A little bit of knowledge can be dangerous. I've seen homes where someone decided that it was important that the ground opening in the receptacle be active, even though there was no ground wire. Therefore, the homeowner ran a wire from the white side of the receptacle (the Neutral) to the screw for the ground wire. This is dangerous and should never be attempted. Unfortunately, using a simple tester like the one suggested here, you won't be able to tell whether the ground is truly connected or "hot-wired" as described here. That's why it always pays to remove receptacles to determine the type of connection.

GFI circuits can be built into a main circuit breaker box or installed locally in place of normal outlets. In a local kitchen installation with several outlets, only one GFI breaker need be installed if the other plugs slave to it. Be sure to check all areas where water is present to be sure that GFI circuit breakers are installed. When checking GFI circuits, be sure that they operate properly.

Operation

To check the operation of a GFI circuit breaker installed in an outlet, place your tester in the Hot and Neutral plugs, and press the Test button. The circuit should break (you'll hear a click, and the Reset button will pop out), and your light should go out. Press Reset to turn the circuit back on.

To check the operation of slave plugs, put the tester into the plug as above, then go back to the GFI breaker and press Test. Your tester light should go out, indicating the slave plug is connected to the GFI circuit. If the GFI breaks but your tester light does not go out, the plug you are testing is not part of the GFI circuit.

Most older homes do not have GFI circuits. You may wish to have them installed as a safety precaution.

Wiring

Most homes have copper wiring, although some have aluminum (see below). The wiring runs through the walls, and the type of insulation used is usually determined by local codes. Some communities require all wire to be sheathed in metal cable. (The individual insulated wire strands run through the cable.) Others allow the use of Romex or some similar self-insulating cable. Here, the individually insulated wires are wrapped in a nonconducting paper, and plastic is wrapped around them. This plastic-sheathed wire is then strung through the walls. I personally prefer Romex because I've seen electricians strip wires when they attempted to run them through metal cables, causing expensive-to-find shorts when the power was turned on.

When examining a home's wiring, check the following:

- Type
- Adequacy
- Condition

Type   Does the home have aluminum or copper wires? To find out, *turn off all the power at the main circuit breaker.* Then go to a light switch, unscrew the cover, remove the two screws holding the switch to its wall box and pull it straight out. There should be enough extra wiring to allow you to move it out a few inches.

Examine the naked wires going into the switch. If the metal is silver-colored, it's aluminum. If it's copper-colored, it's copper. Aluminum is not as good a conductor of electricity as copper, but it costs about half as much; therefore, it's used in some homes. To make up for its lack of conductivity, aluminum wire usually must be thicker than copper wire.

The problem with aluminum is that over time and usage, where it joins outlets, switches, appliances and so forth, it can come loose. The electricity flowing through the aluminum can actually help it unwind from a fitting, and loose fittings can cause arcing (a large spark), which can lead to a fire. Therefore, while there probably is nothing wrong with aluminum in a home, wherever it makes contact with plugs or appliances, an approved connector (sometimes marked "CO/ALR") must be used. If you discover aluminum wiring in the home, have a qualified electrical inspector check it for appropriate connectors. You could save yourself a fire later on. (Note: Even if there is no aluminum at a socket, check the fuse box or circuit breaker. Sometimes aluminum is used for the heavier wires there.)

Adequacy   Is the wiring sufficiently thick to handle all of your household needs? You can easily tell when the wiring is inadequate. For example, you're reading under a lamp, and someone downstairs turns on the dishwasher or garbage disposal. Instantly, your light dims. This is because the wiring is of inadequate size.

Depending on the number of circuits, household wiring will typically be 12-gauge to 16-gauge single-strand wire. For 220 volts, these numbers jump enormously, to between 4-gauge and 8-gauge multistrand wiring.

You can check the wiring when you pull out a plug, as noted above. *(Be sure the power is all off at the main.)* Usually, the gauge will be marked on the wire. The lower the number, the better. Any circuits of more than 16-gauge should be considered suspect.

To truly ensure the adequacy of all wiring, you must determine how many plugs are on a circuit. Usually, you can do this by checking the number of plugs against the number of circuits at the fuse box or circuit breaker box against the gauge of the wiring. Typically, there should be one circuit for every 400 to 500 square feet. This, however, requires the expertise of someone skilled in electrical circuitry to calculate.

You may want to ask the owner about the electrical adequacy and get the owner to sign off on a disclosure statement that no problems exist. (Note: Adding more circuits or increasing the capacity of circuits is like rewiring; it involves cutting into walls, replastering and doing carpentry and electrical work. In short, it's amazingly expensive.)

Condition   Most modern wiring will last (or outlast) the home itself—but not so for older wiring. Modern wiring is sheathed in long-lasting plastic or even metal conduit. But years ago, wiring was sheathed in a kind of rubberized tar coating. While the insulation was adequate, over time (and particularly when exposed to high heat conditions, as often is the case in attics in the summer), the insulation would decay and break off, leaving the naked wires exposed. When this happens, any slight jarring can cross the Hot and Neutral wires, cause arcing and result in a fire.

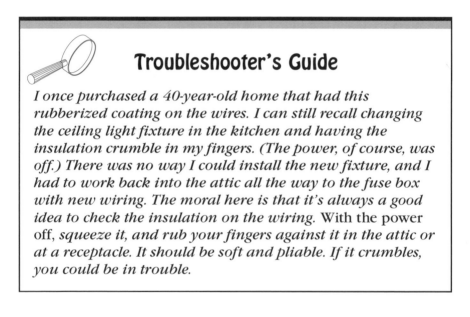

Troubleshooter's Guide

I once purchased a 40-year-old home that had this rubberized coating on the wires. I can still recall changing the ceiling light fixture in the kitchen and having the insulation crumble in my fingers. (The power, of course, was off.) There was no way I could install the new fixture, and I had to work back into the attic all the way to the fuse box with new wiring. The moral here is that it's always a good idea to check the insulation on the wiring. With the power off, *squeeze it, and rub your fingers against it in the attic or at a receptacle. It should be soft and pliable. If it crumbles, you could be in trouble.*

Fuse Box or Circuit Breaker Box

The power from the street enters a home via large wires either from an overhead service or from underground. There are usually three wires, which go directly to the home's main fuse box or circuit breaker box. Here, there is a shut-off for all power, as well as breakers (or fuses) for each circuit (see Figure 8.2). This way, in the event of a short, power is cut off automatically. Of course, you can also turn it off manually.

The three wires coming in are usually two large black wires and a naked third wire (Neutral). In the United States, 110 volts, 60 cycles usually comes in on each of the black wires. When you connect a circuit between one black wire and the Neutral wire, you have 110 volts. If you connect a circuit between both black wires, you combine the power to achieve 220 volts, common for electrical appliances such as stoves, water heaters and dryers.

The fuse box or circuit breaker box connects all the circuits in the home to the main power supply lines coming in. However, wiring itself is usually hidden behind a metal panel. You see only the fuses or the breakers; therefore, you can turn off the power (or turn it back on) safely, without risking shock by touching a live wire. If this protective panel is missing (you see wiring inside the box), contact an electrician before proceeding.

Figure 8.2 Fuse and Circuit Breaker

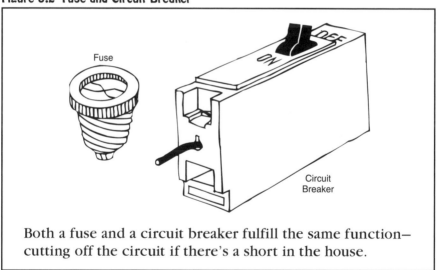

Both a fuse and a circuit breaker fulfill the same function—cutting off the circuit if there's a short in the house.

When examining the fuse box or circuit breaker box, check the following:

- Adequacy
- Operation

Adequacy   As noted earlier, most modern homes have 200-amp service. That is currently deemed necessary to run all of the appliances, the air-conditioning, the heating and so forth. This means that the main circuit breaker in the box can handle a maximum of 200 amps without blowing. The amperage is usually stamped on the main circuit breaker or elsewhere on the box.

A few years ago, 100-amp or even 90-amp service was considered adequate. If the home you are inspecting has this lower level of service, it probably is adequate for the electrical features present at the time the home was built. But if you add air-conditioning, extra appliances, a new room and so on, you'll probably need to put in a new box and new circuits. Unless you handle this yourself, it will cost a minimum of several thousand dollars by the time the wiring is attached and the box populated with circuit breakers.

Operation   Circuit breaker boxes are usually fairly easy to check. Either the power is going through and they're working, or the power is off and they're not.

About the only thing that can go wrong is that a circuit breaker, over time, will weaken and need to be replaced. Circuit breakers weaken if you blow the circuit too often by overloading it (too many appliances in one plug) or sometimes if the wires going into the breaker are loose, causing arcing.

To test a circuit breaker, the power must be on. *Be careful. There's a lot of voltage and amperage here. It's a good idea to have someone experienced check the box first to be sure all of the safety features are in place.* I also suggest you turn on all the lights and appliances in the home so that power flows through the circuits.

Assuming all the circuits work (there are no lights or plugs that don't operate), turn an individual breaker to Off, then switch it back to On. It should catch in the on position and stay there. If it bounces back or won't stay on, you may have a bad breaker. Breakers are usually inexpensive—less than $20—if you can find the right ones for your box. Changing them may require the services of an electrician unless you are familiar with the process. *(Always be sure the power is off at the main breaker.)* Breakers usually have only one wire going in and just pop into and out of the box after the panel is removed. (If you change them, be sure the wire is screwed in tight and that the breaker is securely refitted into the panel.) As I said, you'll be working very close to live wires and electricity. If you're not comfortable doing so, call an electrician.

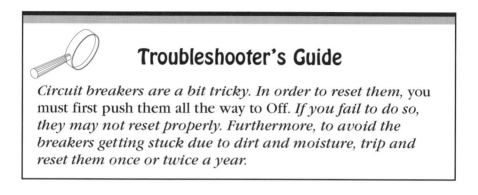

Troubleshooter's Guide

Circuit breakers are a bit tricky. In order to reset them, you must first push them all the way to Off. *If you fail to do so, they may not reset properly. Furthermore, to avoid the breakers getting stuck due to dirt and moisture, trip and reset them once or twice a year.*

Sometimes, when you reset a breaker that has a load on the line, you may hear a pop or even see an arc of electricity. The pop is acceptable; the arc indicates that something may be amiss inside the box. Have an electrician check it out.

Fuse boxes are completely different from circuit breakers. Fuses screw into sockets that are usually, but not always, the same size as light bulb sockets. The fuses themselves typically have a transparent top, showing the fusible material. When too much power runs through the circuit, the fusible link disintegrates, and the fuse blows. The transparent top now typically becomes blackened. You can usually tell a blown fuse with a glance at the box.

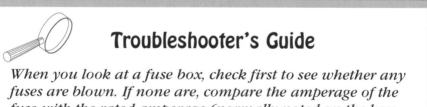

Troubleshooter's Guide

When you look at a fuse box, check first to see whether any fuses are blown. If none are, compare the amperage of the fuse with the rated amperage (normally noted on the box next to the fuse socket). If you detect that a higher amp fuse than rated has been inserted, it suggests that the circuitry in the home is inadequate.

To replace fuses, *turn off the power.* Then simply unscrew the old fuse, and screw in a new one. The trick is to get the right amperage. Each fuse socket should be marked for a specific maximum amperage—for example, 15 amps or 20 amps. If fuses blow too often, it means too many electrical items draw power off the circuit. The solution is to unplug something. Most people, however, either don't want the inconvenience or own a home where there simply aren't enough circuits to meet household needs. Therefore, they put a higher amperage fuse in. This won't blow as readily; however, it means that the wiring is now taking more amperage than it may be rated for. Raising the fuse amperage above what is called for may be trading an inconvenience for a fire.

Telephone and Cable Wiring

In addition to the standard electrical service, modern homes are also wired for telephone and television cable. These wires carry a very low voltage and, as a result, we are not usually concerned with them. Nevertheless, they should be grounded so they don't pose a hazard. For example, if you drop the phone in the bath and the phone isn't grounded, you could be electrocuted. (You could be electrocuted in any event, but with a grounded phone, your chances are far better.)

Both the phone and the cable lines are grounded, usually where they enter the home. They may be grounded by using a bare wire attached to the cold water plumbing. This used to be the traditional method of grounding, but today it is less favored, and a grounding rod, driven deep into the ground, is more often used. In a better installation, both telephone and cable enter the home at the fuse box or circuit breaker box and are grounded to it.

When troubleshooting telephone and cable wiring, check for the following:

• Grounding

• Location

Underground Wiring

Finally, one aspect of the electrical system that few people consider, yet that can be unbearably costly, is converting from overhead electrical service to underground. Newer areas are mainly underground these days; older areas are above ground, with wires strung on telephone poles. Problems occur when local governing agencies determine that it's time to switch from overhead to underground. They may require a bond that you must pay off over many years. Depending on the distance and the difficulty of going underground, the costs could be as high as $10,000 or more!

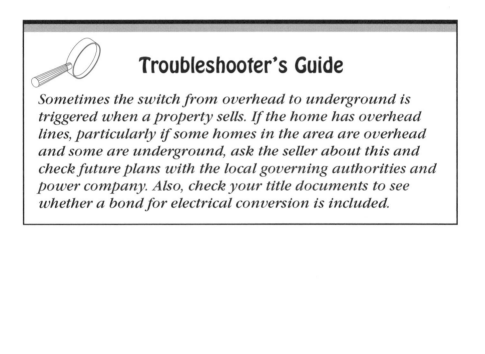

Troubleshooter's Guide

Sometimes the switch from overhead to underground is triggered when a property sells. If the home has overhead lines, particularly if some homes in the area are overhead and some are underground, ask the seller about this and check future plans with the local governing authorities and power company. Also, check your title documents to see whether a bond for electrical conversion is included.

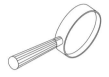

Heating and Cooling System Concerns

LIKE the plumbing and electrical systems, the heater and air conditioner are vital to any home—and they can be expensive to fix if they break down. A thorough home inspection will include an examination of these for problems.

Heating Systems

We'll start with heaters, but because there are so many different types with different potential problems, we'll cover each type of heater separately. Probably the most popular in the country is the forced-air heater.

Forced-Air System

In a forced-air system, a central furnace uses oil or gas (usually natural gas, but propane is also widely used) to heat air, which is then forced through ducts by a fan until it is blown out in the various rooms of the home. The system works very efficiently in that you can raise the temperature in a cold home extremely quickly. We used to own a home in the mountains with a high efficiency forced-air furnace that, in winter, could raise the air temperature 40 degrees in less than an hour!

The trouble with forced air is that particles of dust are always being blown around, which means that it's necessary to constantly change the filter; once a month is recommended in winter. Also, forced air is not very good at radiant heating. It quickly warms the air in a room but slowly warms the walls, furniture and floors. Thus, in very cold climates, while the air temperature may be a pleasant 70 degrees, the walls could be a much cooler 50 degrees. As a result, as soon as the desired air temperature is reached and the heater turns off, the walls begin cooling the air, requiring the heater to come on again.

Virtually all forced-air furnaces operate on a thermostat. It should go without saying that you will want to turn the thermostat on and off (all the way to high, then to low) several times to see that the heater works. If the heater goes on and off, both the thermostat and the control valve in the furnace are probably functioning properly. If the heater does not cycle on, the thermostat may need to be replaced. A standard thermostat for heat costs only about $50. A control valve can be less than $100, uninstalled.

When checking a forced-air heater, look for the following:

- Height of ducts

- Condition of ductwork

- Cleanliness of fan motor

- Operation of heat exchanger

- Ventilation of heater

Height of Ducts   Heat naturally rises, so in an ideal situation, the ducts bringing forced air into a room would be in the floor. The warm air would be blown across the room at the lowest possible level, then allowed to rise slowly.

The problem is that in many homes, the ducts are located high on the walls or in the ceilings. This is excellent for air-conditioning because cold air blown out is forced down by hot air rising. But for heating, the warm air blown out tends to stay in the top two-thirds of the room. The bottom third can be uncomfortably cold.

Condition of Ductwork   Years ago, ductwork was almost entirely made of sheetmetal, meticulously hand-crafted to fit a home and hung in place piece by piece. The trouble was that the ductwork was sometimes not insulated, so hot air leaving the furnace was often cool or barely warm by the time it reached distant rooms.

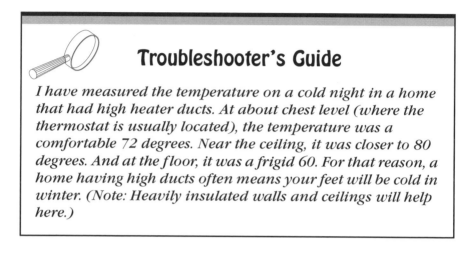

Troubleshooter's Guide

I have measured the temperature on a cold night in a home that had high heater ducts. At about chest level (where the thermostat is usually located), the temperature was a comfortable 72 degrees. Near the ceiling, it was closer to 80 degrees. And at the floor, it was a frigid 60. For that reason, a home having high ducts often means your feet will be cold in winter. (Note: Heavily insulated walls and ceilings will help here.)

When inspecting ductwork in a home (you can see the ductwork in the attic or in the crawlspace or basement from underneath), check to see that metal pipes are insulated. Good insulation is heavy and thick, usually made of layers of fiberglass. Poor or no insulation shows bare metal or sometimes painted metal ducts. If you're not sure, turn on the heater, let it run awhile and feel the ducts. If they're warm or hot, they're losing heat. If they're cool, they're well insulated. If the ducts are not insulated, your heating bills will be significantly higher, and you will have less heat in winter. Changing ducts can be fairly expensive, though not as costly as in the past.

Today, ductwork in homes is mostly strung fiberglass tubing. Fiberglass is pressed between two pieces of plastic and wound around a metal coil much like a Slinky toy. It can be stretched or compressed to fit long or short runs. It can be cut easily. And because the walls of the ductwork are actually fiberglass, it conserves heat very well. The trouble is, it can be damaged easily. Check for tears, holes and gaps in strung fiberglass ducts.

Finally, check all of the grills where forced air enters a room. They should be clean, unobstructed, operating and well attached. Over the years, they will sometimes break, which means you won't be able to direct the air where you want it to go or to close it off. Sometimes people remove the grills when painting, then set them back up, ready to fall off. They need to be secured, usually by at least two long screws. They also need to be clean, with the vents unobstructed, so the air can escape. I've seen grills that were so dirty it was easier to replace them than to clean them. (Grills are relatively inexpensive, assuming they are a standard size, costing less than $20 apiece.)

Troubleshooter's Guide

I once had a pup who was very high-strung. I had to go out for a few hours, so I left him in the basement of my home. While I was gone, he somehow managed to tear down the fiberglass ducting for nearly half the rooms in my home, chewing it into hundreds of pieces. (Fortunately, he didn't seem to swallow any of it or get ill.) I learned an expensive lesson both about my dog and about plastic and fiberglass ductwork!

Cleanliness of Fan Motor   The fan motor is the heart of a forced-air system. Such motors are usually about one horsepower or more, and they turn a cylindrical high-speed fan, usually by means of a belt similar to a car's fan belt.

Fan motors are probably the most neglected appliance in a home. They may go unchecked for a dozen years. Most are built, in fact, to never be serviced. (That doesn't mean they don't need servicing; it just means that there are no service points built in.)

Assuming that the belts are not too tight, these motors tend to last and last, until the bearings run out of oil. In older motors, you can oil the bearings through special, almost impossible to reach, fittings. Newer motors tend to be sealed.

When the bearings are starting to wear, a motor will often produce a hum or sometimes a squeal. Eventually, the motor will begin to overheat, then burn out. To test it, run the motor without the heater on. (Usually, there's a Fan Only switch either near the motor or at the thermostat.) Listen closely. You should hear only a very minor purr. Any loud noise at all indicates problems. A new motor typically costs between $100 and $200, uninstalled.

Operation of Heat Exchanger   If the motor is the heart of the heating system, the heat exchanger is the lungs. In a forced-air furnace, burned gas generating heat is directed at a hollow core lung of metal. On the outside of the lung, the burned gas along with all of its combustibles, including carbon monoxide, pass across the metal, heating that metal, then continue on up into the vent and into the air outside. On the inside of the lung, however, air from the home is ducted in, heated, then ducted back to the home.

Thus, the heat exchanger has two completely separate air sources. Inside, it is the clean, heated air from the home. Outside, it is the hot flames from the burning gas and the exhaust. The metal core exchanges the heat from the outside to the inside while never allowing the two to mix. If they were to mix, noxious and deadly fumes could be pumped into the home. Therein, of course, lies the problem.

Over time and with the burning of some types of fuels, the heat exchanger will develop leaks. These can be tiny pinpricks or substantial holes (see Figure 9.1). Any holes in the heat exchanger are dangerous and require immediate replacement. Quite frankly, a heat exchanger costs almost as much as a new furnace, so when the exchanger goes, I usually opt to buy a new furnace. New gas blower furnaces usually cost from $1,200 on up. You have a variety of ways to detect holes in the heat exchanger, most of which require you to be an expert. We'll consider two that don't. On the other hand, most utility companies automatically check the heat exchanger whenever they turn on the heater after it has been off. If you turn off your heater and call in the utility (usually a free service), the utility professional can quickly check it for you.

With the thermostat inside the home set to its lowest register, remove the outer panels of the heater so that you can see the pilot light and the burners below. *(Be careful. Don't get too close.)* Now have someone in the home turn up the thermostat. When this happens, the burners ignite and begin heating the exchanger. However, because the exchanger is initially filled with cold air, the fan doesn't normally start up right away. Now watch the

Figure 9.1 Heat Exchanger Showing Hole

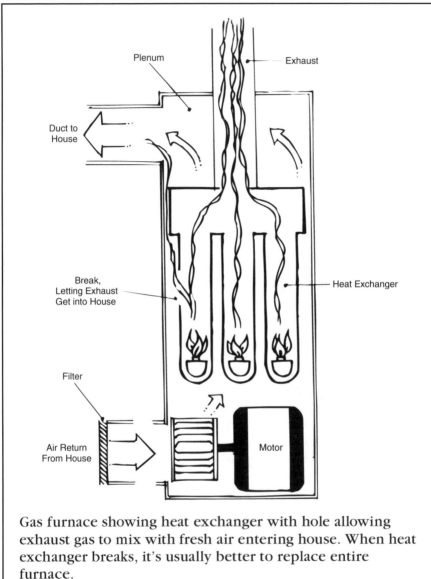

Gas furnace showing heat exchanger with hole allowing exhaust gas to mix with fresh air entering house. When heat exchanger breaks, it's usually better to replace entire furnace.

flames until the fan starts. When it does so, air quickly begins moving inside (but not outside) the heat exchanger. Because the flames are all outside, they should not be affected by the fan going on unless there's a hole in the exchanger. Then you'll see the flames suddenly sucked up as the fan sucks in air from the outside to the inside of the exchanger. This may last a few moments. with the flames dying back, or may continue. Either way, it's a sign that there's a problem. Have the exchanger checked by a professional.

The second method of detecting holes in the heat exchanger is to place some particularly odorous material on the outside of the exchanger. I usually use a dollop of oil paint. When the furnace comes on, if the exchanger is functional, the paint will quickly be burned away to the outside. If the exchanger has a hole, however, some of the paint fumes will be sucked through, and you'll be able to smell burned paint in the home. (To enhance the effect, close most of the ducts, then stand by the ones remaining open.) If you smell the odor, the exchanger is probably bad.

To be completely sure about the heat exchanger, a visual inspection is necessary. However, because the exchanger is located so deep in the furnace, this usually can be done only by an expert using a flashlight and a mirror.

When in doubt, let an expert check the heat exchanger.

Ventilation of Heater   One other area to consider that is related to burning gas is the vent on top of the furnace. All gas furnaces must be vented. However, sometimes people bump the vent, and sometimes the vent is installed improperly.

Visually inspect the vent to be sure that it is intact and has no holes. Furthermore, the vent should have at least a foot of air space surrounding it so that heat expelled from the vent won't ignite a wall. Finally, there should be no combustible materials, especially newspapers and paint thinner, anywhere near a gas furnace.

(Note: Some advanced furnaces, such as the Lennox Pulse and the Amana, burn so efficiently that they really don't need a vent and instead use regular PVC pipe to duct burned gases to the outside. On the other hand, these furnaces tend to produce water as a byproduct and rust can be a problem. Check it out.)

Gravity Feed System

Another kind of furnace that is not found much today—called a gravity feed heater—looks just like a forced-air unit, only it has no fan. In addition, the ducts are nearly twice as large. This unit must be located in a basement because it operates on the principle that heat rises. Burners heat an exchanger, and the air inside the exchanger rises naturally through the large ducts into the home.

Gravity feed furnaces have the advantage of not blowing air and dust around the home. On the other hand, the ducts are usually metal, and they make a great deal of noise expanding and contracting.

The trouble with these types of furnaces is that the heat exchanger is very heavy-duty, and when it goes, it is prohibitively expensive to replace. Therefore, most gravity feed furnaces that burn out are replaced with forced air units.

If the home has a gravity feed furnace that is old, I would just assume that sometime within the next few years it will have to be replaced with a forced-air unit. (Usually, the ductwork is replaced at the same time, making the job even more expensive.)

Electric System

Generally speaking, electric heating is the least efficient and most costly system you can get, although there is a way to save money with the system, as we'll discuss shortly.

Built-in electric heat usually comes in the form of radiant or fan-blown baseboard panels. Although radiant electric panels can be placed in floors and ceilings, these are far less common. The baseboard panels are easily and cheaply installed (the main reason many builders use them). Typically, they require about 10 to 30 watts per square foot of living area (assuming a normal 8-foot ceiling) to adequately heat a room.

The cost of electric heating is normally far more than the cost of heat from any other source. However, it is often possible to install a separate thermostat in every room. Thus, instead of heating an entire home, you can heat only a bedroom, a living room or a section of the home. Thus, although the per-unit cost of electric heat is higher, by leaving the heat off in most of the home, you can actually reduce costs over a forced-air system, which heats the entire indoor area.

When troubleshooting an electric heating system, check for the following:

- Adequacy

- Burned wiring

Adequacy If you buy a home with electric heating, be sure that the system will actually heat the home. The best way to check is to walk through the home on a cold day. Barring that, make sure that the heater has enough wattage for the area (see above) and that the heaters actually do get warm and send out heat.

Troubleshooter's Guide

I once had some friends who installed baseboard heating in a home that was essentially an open, two-story "great room." The heater had enough wattage per square foot of home but because of the height of the ceiling and the lack of proper wall insulation, they never could get the place warm on a cold night. In fact, I can recall being in their home and placing my hand on the heater only to find that, though operating, the heater itself was cold! Check with the owners and get them to sign off on their disclosure statement that the heating system will adequately maintain an acceptable temperature (usually 72 degrees) on the coldest nights.

Burned Wiring The wiring that brings electricity to the heater must be of sufficient size that the wiring itself does not heat up because of the heater's resistance. Sometimes too small a wire is selected. When this is the case, you can often tell by examining the wiring where it enters the heater. (This is usually at or near one end; you will probably have to remove the cover panel.) The insulation should be flexible and intact. A small amount of discoloration may have occurred from proximity to the heater elements, but severe discoloration, burn marks or deterioration suggests inadequate wiring or other problems with the heater. Have an electrician inspect it further.

Wood-Burning Stoves

In many areas of the country, particularly where the temperature falls below freezing in winter, people have installed wood-burning stoves. Sometimes these are freestanding, and other times, they are inserted into an existing fireplace. These, naturally enough, are called inserts.

Wood-burning stoves are far more efficient than fireplaces, though far less efficient than almost any other heat source. A high-tech wood-burning stove today rarely can achieve 50 percent efficiency (half the energy goes into heating the home; the other half is lost). Compare this to a high-tech gas furnace, which can achieve as much as 95 percent efficiency.

The advantages of wood-burning stoves are that the fuel source is often inexpensive (wood) and that the radiant heat they produce is often very soothing, although it tends to dry things out.

Always be sure that the stove rests on a noncombustible base (not a wood floor or carpet but stones, bricks or the like) and that it is an approved distance from walls and other combustibles. (Often the stoves will have a sticker saying how close they can be placed to walls.)

Troubleshooter's Guide

I have a wood-burning stove in my home. I find the heat it produces far superior to the heat from any other source, and watching the flames through the glass door on a cold winter night is often better than watching television!

The trouble with wood-burning stoves is that they are a strong source of pollution. A lot of stoves burning on a cold night with no wind can make the air outside almost unbreathable. As a consequence, state governments have begun regulating wood-burning stoves. In many areas, owners are not allowed to burn them on certain nights. Also, only certain types of stoves that meet strict standards can be sold, and those standards are getting more rigid each year. It would appear that in a few years, stoves that burn raw wood may be prohibited, and only pellet stoves—those that burn a processed wood pellet—may be allowed in many areas.

When inspecting a wood-burning stove, look for the following:

- Cracks, broken fire bricks, broken glass, a loose or missing door insulator

- Clean flue

- Approval sticker

Cracks, Broken Fire Stacks, Broken Glass, a Loose or Missing Door Insulator   This heading pretty much speaks for itself. If any of the metal is cracked, chances are the stove will need to be replaced. Fire bricks (located inside the stove) are inexpensive and can be replaced easily. A broken door glass must be replaced before a fire can be started. Its price will vary with the type of stove but usually will cost $100 or more. A door insulator probably can be replaced for under $25.

Clean Flue   A wood-burning stove generates so much soot and creosote that it will sometimes catch fire. A flue fire can threaten a home. Always insist that a wood-burning stove's flue be cleaned when you buy a home. Thereafter, a cleaning at least once a year is usually recommended. There are also certain procedures for burning wood and certain types of wood that will help keep the flue clean.

Approval Sticker   Modern wood stoves contain stickers indicating that they meet government standards as of a certain date. If the stove you inspect has no sticker, question the owner. It may turn out the stove was installed without a permit and, therefore, might be illegal.

(Note: When a wood-burning stove is replaced, it is usually necessary to get a permit from the local building and safety department. This can present a problem if the authority requires an approved stove, which can cost a great deal of money (typically $2,000 and up). In some cases, the locale may prohibit wood-burning stoves, and replacement may be impossible.)

Wall Heaters

Wall heaters are usually gas or electric panels set into a wall to heat a home. They are not very efficient, but they do produce a lot of heat, though in a localized area. They should be placed so that a person walking by is unlikely to touch them and get burned.

If the wall heater is gas, check for the same sorts of things as with a forced-air gas furnace—that the thermostat works and that there are no holes in the heat exchanger. For an electric panel, check the same sorts of things as noted earlier for the baseboard heater—burned wires and adequacy.

Steam Heat System

Some older homes have boilers and pipes that carry steam to radiators in every room. This system should not be confused with the modern hot water system discussed next.

Steam heat is actually quite a good system because it adds moisture, as well as heat, to the air. Unfortunately, the radiators sometimes get too hot and can result in burns, particularly to children. Also, these systems tend to use asbestos as insulation, which may pose a serious health hazard. (Removing asbestos requires experts and is extremely expensive.) Finally, the boilers themselves are inherently dangerous and, if safety systems fail, could cause an explosion.

If a home you inspect has a steam heat system, do not attempt to examine it yourself. Call in a heating expert for an evaluation.

Hot Water System

In a hot water system, water is heated either electrically or by gas, then is pumped through insulated copper pipes to baseboard radiators in all rooms of the home. (It also could be pumped to panels under the floors or in the ceilings.)

The hot water radiates heat efficiently. The problem is that it takes a long time to raise the temperature in a room by this means—sometimes several days if the temperature is quite cold. On the other hand, once a desired temperature is obtained, it can be maintained accurately. Hot water systems usually allow an owner to partition the home and heat only the sections the owner desires.

When checking a home's hot water system, look for signs of the following:

- Leaks

- Worn pump, motor and valves

- Worn heater

Leaks   A hot water system will last almost indefinitely unless it develops leaks. Usually, these are found around the pump, but they may occur anywhere. If a leak develops in a panel under a floor or in an attic, it could be very messy and expensive to fix. On the other hand, if there's a leak to an exposed pipe, it can usually be fixed quite easily and quickly by a plumber or by anyone able to solder copper pipe.

Worn Pump, Motor and Valves   The weakest link in this system is the pump. It usually must be oiled regularly. If it is not maintained, it will burn out. Listen to the pump. It should hum smoothly. Any whining or other loud noise suggests a worn pump that may need to be replaced soon. Also, inspect the pump visually. It should be clean, with no water or oil stains. Water stains suggest leaking, and oil stains indicate a worn pump.

Similarly, a motor should hum quietly. Beware of any whining or loud noises. It may be difficult to tell whether the problem is the pump or the motor, because they are so closely linked. Therefore, if you suspect any problem, have a heating expert check it out.

Valves are either manual or electrically operated and control the flow of heat to individual rooms, as well as to sections of the home. They rarely fail, but when they do, they must be replaced. Check for ease of movement and leaks.

Worn Heater   The hot water system uses a heater to warm the water. To check it for problems, see the "Heater" section in Chapter 7.

Oil Furnace

The oil furnace is usually a forced-air type of furnace; however, the fuel supply is oil. This system is not efficient and produces a lot of soot. However, the fuel oil it uses is often quite inexpensive.

On your inspection of an oil furnace, check for the following:

- Storage adequacy

- Oil leaks

- Water corrosion

Storage Adequacy   The oil furnace requires a storage tank, typically available in sizes from 250 gallons on up. Usually, the larger the size the better because there is less chance of it running out of oil during a storm and you can often buy oil at a lower unit cost because of the amount you are purchasing.

Oil Leaks   Look for oil stains under the tank or in the line running from the tank to the heater. If there's a tank leak, fixing it may be more expensive than replacing the tank, but either is an expensive proposition. Oil leaks in the line running from the tank to the heater are troublesome but relatively inexpensive to fix.

Water Corrosion   It's important that the oil level be kept up in the tank. If it's allowed to be low for long periods of time, water will evaporate out of the oil and corrode the inside of the tank. This corrosion will then fall back into the oil and plug the filter in front of the furnace.

The way to check for water corrosion is to examine the oil filter. However, that's a messy task, and usually you won't have time to do it. As an alternative, look to see whether there is a lot of fresh oil under the filter, suggesting that it is changed quite often. A filter that is changed often indicates problems in the tank. If you suspect problems, have an experienced oil furnace professional check the unit.

Air-Conditioning

Air-conditioning is no longer considered an extra in much of the country but a necessity. There are two types of air-conditioning: the Swamp Cooler, used primarily in the Southwest, and the true air conditioner. The Swamp Cooler is actually a large water radiator, usually placed on the roof, that cools air flowing through it by the evaporation of water pumped over a grill. (When water evaporates, it absorbs heat and, therefore, cools.) The cool air is then sent by ducts into the home.

About the only things that go wrong with Swamp Coolers are leaks and motor burnout. You may have to get on the roof to check out the cooling unit. Look under the "Forced-Air System" section in this chapter for tips on inspecting the motor.

True air-conditioning involves a radiator, a compressor, an expansion valve and a coil and operates just like a refrigerator.

The radiator and compressor are typically located outside, while the coil and expansion valve are inside, next to a fan (usually in the forced-air furnace.) When you turn on the air conditioner, heat from the home is ducted over the coils, which absorb the heat, then transfer it so that it can be radiated outside.

To check the air conditioner, turn it on. You should feel cool air coming out of the vents. Keep in mind that most home air conditioning units cannot easily cool down a home that is already hot. They simply don't have enough capacity. Rather, they can maintain a cool temperature in a home that hasn't yet heated up. Thus, the air coming out of the vents should be cold but may not be icy. If the air doesn't feel cold, the air conditioner may not be functioning and should be checked by an air-conditioning service person.

Also, the blower outside should be quiet. If it makes a lot of noise when operating, either the motor or the compressor could be ready to fail. Have an expert check it out.

There really aren't any other easy methods of checking out an air conditioner because it's basically a sealed unit. It takes a professional to pressure test the line and examine the coil and other elements.

Fireplace Cautions

A fireplace is almost a requirement for most homes these days. It's what marketing people call a seller; that is, it helps sell the property.

Unfortunately, while most people like the idea of logs snapping and crackling in the hearth on a cold winter's day, a fireplace is actually quite low-tech and impractical. Fireplaces date back not only centuries but millennia, to the days of castles, when it was thought that the only way to get warmth was to have a fireplace in every room. Yet, as those ancients never seemed to figure out, the rooms always were somehow colder with a fire roaring in a fireplace.

The truth is that a fire consumes great amounts of air. Where does this air come from? It comes in through cracks and seams in the home; it comes in from outside. Thus, when your fireplace roars, the fire is actually pulling in large amounts of cold air from outside. The cold air goes right to the fire, which heats it and immediately sends it up the chimney. Therefore, you are warmed by radiant heat when you sit in front of the fireplace, but the home grows colder as air is sucked in from outside. That's why people in the old days used to complain that their feet were roasting but their backs were freezing when sitting in front of a fireplace.

You can reduce the problem in several ways. Adding a wood-burning stove insert will almost cure it. Putting a glass screen in front of the fireplace to control the air flow will help a lot. Judiciously closing the damper part way will also help, but it could result in smoke entering the home if the fire gets too strong (or the draw isn't sufficient).

In any event, if you inspect a home with a fireplace, give it a plus for a glass screen, an operative damper and a wood stove insert. If it doesn't offer these, you may want to give it a minus because you'll probably want to buy one or more of the items yourself.

Figure 10.1 illustrates the elements of a fireplace where problems can occur. When inspecting a fireplace, ask yourself the following questions:

- Does the damper work?

- Does it draw? Does it smoke?

- Does it have a spark arrestor?

- Are there any cracked bricks outside or inside?

- Are there water leaks where it goes through the ceiling?

- Is the hearth sagging?

Does the Damper Work?

The damper is located inside the chimney and can close it completely. It's made of metal, and it operates by a handle that hangs down into the fireplace opening. By manipulating the handle, you can open or close the damper.

When you inspect the damper, wear old clothes (and, of course, be sure that there's no fire). Get inside the fireplace so you can look up. Wear safety glasses.

Now operate the damper handle, and push open the damper. If the fireplace has a straight flue, you should be able to see daylight (assuming, of course, that it's daytime) when you look up. With it closed, you should see only blackness. If the flue is not straight, use a flashlight. You should be able to actually see the damper open and close when you work the handle.

If the damper doesn't work, it might only be stuck from lack of use, or it might be broken. Getting it unstuck usually means forcing it a bit. If, on the other hand, it's broken, you'll need to get a contractor in to see about fixing or replacing it. The cost could vary greatly, depending on the problem. (Sometimes just a bolt is missing; other times the fireplace flue has cracked or shifted, freezing the damper in place, and the entire fireplace might need to be replaced.)

Figure 10.1 Fireplace Showing Damper, Lintel, Mantel and Other Problem Areas

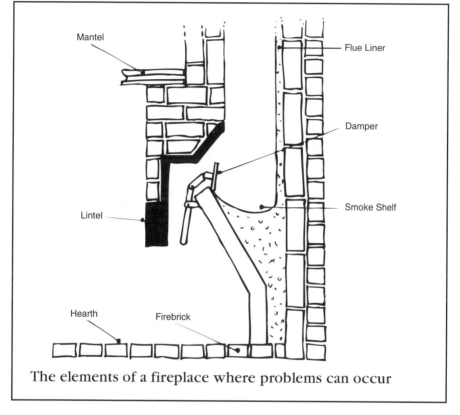

Mantel

Flue Liner

Damper

Smoke Shelf

Lintel

Hearth

Firebrick

The elements of a fireplace where problems can occur

Does It Draw? Does It Smoke?

A good fireplace sucks up the smoke and combustibles from the flames and feeds them up the chimney to the outside. The better designed the fireplace, the stronger the draw and the less smoke produced.

Usually, you can tell whether a fireplace has problems with its draw by looking at the inside ceiling around it. If the ceiling is discolored with smoke, the fireplace probably has problems. Of course, if the ceiling is fresh and clean, it might only mean that the owner has recently painted it. If that's the case, the only real way to judge the draw is to light a fire.

You must ask permission to light a fire. An owner may know the fireplace is bad and may refuse your request. If you light a fire in a bad fireplace without asking permission, you could cause serious smoke damage in the home.

Be sure the damper is fully open before lighting a fire. Also, be aware that any fireplace will not draw well and will smoke a bit when the flue is cold. Once it warms up, it will work better. (Open a window slightly to get a draft up the flue if you have a problem.) Once the fire is going, all the flames and smoke should be evacuated out through the flue.

Troubleshooter's Guide

Sometimes it's hard to know when the flue is open and when it is closed. About the only way to tell, if you don't know from experience, is to look inside, as noted above. I once visited some friends and made the mistake of thinking the flue was fully open when it was fully closed. I started a fire, which got burning quite well before I realized the smoke was going into the home instead of up the chimney. Needless to say, the results were unpleasant. The smoke set off the smoke alarms and made the place generally uninhabitable for several hours. I'll never repeat that mistake, and I hope my warning will prevent you from making the mistake in the first place!

If the fireplace doesn't draw and it smokes, it is possible that the flue is clogged. Having it cleaned may help appreciably. Beyond that, however, the flue may simply be designed badly. (Check to see that the top of the fireplace chimney is higher than the highest ridge point of the roof. If it's not, downdrafts of air could be the problem.)

Does It Have a Spark Arrestor?

Under normal use, sparks from whatever is burning in a fireplace will rise up the chimney. If allowed to escape, they may travel on the wind and set the home's (or another home's) roof on fire. Therefore, it is vital that a spark arrestor be positioned at the top of the fireplace chimney.

A spark arrestor looks like a box made of closely knit wire mesh. It allows heat and air to escape easily but catches burning particles that are bigger than about a quarter-inch or so across. They burn out against the arrestor, then usually drift through harmlessly. A spark arrestor is a must for any fireplace.

Are There Any Cracked Bricks Outside or Inside?

Most fireplaces are built of bricks. When new, the bricks should be unbroken, and the mortar holding them together should be tight and without cracks. Over time, however, either because of shifts in the earth (a big problem in earthquake country) or because the fireplace walls are too thin and the fire overheats them, the bricks and mortar may crack. When that happens, the chimney might be in danger of toppling over, and flames and heat from inside are in danger of escaping, possibly into the walls of the home.

Carefully look at the bricks both on the front of the fireplace and on the exterior. Check the mortar in several places with a screwdriver by poking it hard. It should be resistant, perhaps chip a bit, but that's all.

If cracks are present (particularly diagonal cracks running long distances) or if the mortar is loose or easily dislodged (particularly if you're in earthquake country or it's an old fireplace), you could have a serious problem. Have a contractor check the chimney for structural integrity. Also have a chimney sweep check the inside of the chimney to be sure the insert is intact.

Most fireplaces, in addition to the brick exterior, have an insert that runs the entire height of the chimney. This insert may be made of special fireclay or metal. Sometimes when the bricks on the outside crack, the insert remains intact, meaning the fireplace is probably still safe. However, other times the crack will run all the way through, meaning that flames, heat and gases can escape. In this case, and the fireplace is not safe. About the only way to tell is to actually crawl up into the fireplace and inspect it with a bright light. As I said, call a chimney sweep. He or she will usually perform this service for a relatively small amount of money.

(Note: Some states now insist that metal flue inserts be placed in fireplaces, sometimes when a home changes ownership. If it's an older home, determine whether such a law exists, because inserts can be expensive.)

Now check the mantel and lintel. The mantel is the board or bricks that run across the front of the fireplace. The lintel is a heavy piece of steel right behind the mantel that holds up the front bricks of the fireplace. If the mantel sags, there's probably a problem with the lintel. You may have to get down and look up or even crawl up behind the lintel to see whether there's any problem. A sagging lintel almost always will have cracked bricks. This is a serious problem and may require reconstruction of part or all of the fireplace.

One last check should be the firebricks. In most fireplaces, the bricks surrounding the fire are special. They are built to handle heat extremes. If they are cracked or pieces of them are missing, the fireplace heat can travel directly to the less durable exterior bricks and possibly cause a fire. If the firebricks are in bad shape, they will need to be replaced.

Are There Water Leaks Where It Goes Through the Ceiling?

Fireplaces often go right through the ceiling of a room, through the attic and out the roof. The problem with this is that these fire-places are built from the ground (or at least the floor) up and often are not well attached to the roof. Thus, over the years, the home might sag and lean one way while the fireplace sags and leans another. As a result, when it rains, water can seep in between the fireplace and the roof and leak down onto the ceiling below. Leaks at fireplaces, in fact, are probably the most common leak complaint.

To check for leaks, look at the ceiling where it meets the fireplace chimney. Is there any discoloration from water? If so, there probably is, or was, a leak.

Next check the fireplace as it travels through the attic. Can you see light coming in next to the fireplace? (In some cases, there are actually cracks inches wide.) Are there discolorations or indications of water leakage?

Normally, fixing leakage problems means nothing more than adding new flashing to the fireplace and the roof. A good roofer can do it in less than an hour and for a reasonable price. In some cases, however, leakage indicates a leaning fireplace, which might be a much more serious structural problem and might need to be torn down.

Is the Hearth Sagging?

In some homes, the hearth, or bottom, of the fireplace is built right on the ground. If that's the case, there really isn't any problem because there's cement and ground underneath.

In other cases, however, heavy plywood and then cement and firebricks are laid on the floor of the room. Over time, the enormous weight of the fireplace and chimney can distend the hearth until it sags, causing cracked bricks and holding the potential for a collapsed fireplace.

Look at the hearth. If you can't tell by sight, use a short level to determine whether it's flat. If it sags, get underneath and check the beams holding up the fireplace. Typically, there will be extra supports there but perhaps not. It may be the case that you'll have to put in the extra supports to beef up the floor of the fireplace. This is not particularly costly, but it does take someone with carpentry skills. If the sagging is severe, you may also need to replace some of the firebricks in the hearth.

In general, the fireplace is a wonderful psychological invention but not such a wonderful practical invention. Generally speaking, if it appears that the owners use the fireplace regularly—a lot of wood stored nearby, some smoke stains around the edges of the hearth and on the mantel and a lot of ashes inside—it's probably a good fireplace. Be wary of a fireplace that's spotless and looks as if it's never used. Maybe the owners are just fastidious about keeping it clean. Or maybe they know something about its operation that keeps them from using it.

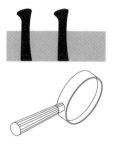

Insulation Inadequacies

IN cold weather country, insulation has always been a necessity. I can recall looking in the attic of a 100-year-old home in Minneapolis and discovering that it had been insulated with what looked like old newspapers. This was not exactly fire-safe but probably not bad insulation for its day.

In warm weather climates, however, such as the Southwest and other parts of the country, insulation is a relatively new thing. As recently as 20 years ago, many homes were built with no insulation at all. The feeling at the time was that energy was cheap, so it made financial sense to pour the money into bigger heaters and air conditioners rather than into insulation. Even when it became customary to insulate, often only the ceilings were done, leaving no insulation in walls or floors.

Today, of course, that has all changed. Almost every new home built anywhere in the country is well insulated with a variety of materials. The challenge for the home inspection, therefore, is to determine, first, whether the home is insulated (usually not a concern with newer properties) and, second, whether the insulation is adequate.

Retrofitting

Before we get to the actual inspection checks, let's consider what it costs to retrofit insulation into an existing home that either has none or has inadequate insulation. If the home has an attic, it's a relatively simple and inexpensive process to blow in a fiberglass or a rock-wool insulation material. Often it can be done to a depth of 12 inches, providing excellent insulation. This, however, covers only the attic. If the home has no attic, it is usually necessary to add much more expensive rigid insulation (usually fiberglass sheets) either directly under or directly over the roof, then install a new ceiling or reshingle—quite an expensive proposition.

Insulating the walls is a totally different story. Some methods include cutting small, round holes in the walls, then either blowing in fiberglass insulation or pouring in a chemical insulator that expands inside the walls. Unfortunately, the holes then must be patched and the walls replastered and painted—again, quite an expensive job.

Another method—perhaps even more expensive—is to add rigid insulation to the existing walls on the inside, then cover that with another layer of plasterboard.

Insulating the floors (usually necessary only in cold climates) can be done easily if there's a basement or crawlspace underneath. If there's a slab, it's impossible (but often unnecessary) to insulate the floors.

Given the problems with retrofitting insulation, it's very important that you inspect a home carefully to determine whether it is insulated.

When inspecting a home's insulation, consider the following:

- Whether or where the home is insulated

- R-rating of insulation

- Insulation of windows and doors

Whether and Where the Home Is Insulated

There are three areas you need to check: the attic, walls and floors. The attic should be easy. Every attic has a crawlspace. Using a ladder (and being careful not to fall), remove the cover and climb up into the attic. (You don't necessarily have to climb all the way into the attic, just high enough to see inside.) Take a look around. Either the insulation should be laid carefully in sheets between the rafters or it should be blown evenly throughout. If, from the attic, you can see the rafters and the sheetrock or plaster on top of the ceiling with nothing on it, there's no attic insulation. (Note: If you climb into an attic that has insulation, particularly rock wool, wear protective clothing and an adequate air filtration mask.)

Troubleshooter's Guide

About 15 to 30 years ago, it was common to spray insulation onto a a home's ceilings. It wasn't much, but the idea was that the material would insulate somewhat. Unfortunately, an asbestos compound was frequently used. If a home is more than ten years old, be suspicious of blown-in ceilings (they look as though they have a thin layer of popcorn on them). It takes an expert to check, but if the insulation is asbestos, this could constitute a health hazard.

As of this writing, I know of no government requirements that such ceilings be checked or fixed, but such regulations will certainly come in the future. With millions of homes having this type of ceiling, it is sure to be an enormous undertaking. To remove an asbestos blown-on ceiling requires workpeople wearing special breathing apparatus and clothes and having the home sealed so the asbestos does not escape into the outside environment. The cost is enormous. On the other hand, it seems to be the case that as long as this type of ceiling is not disturbed, the level of asbestos in the air is relatively small. Therefore, some owners have sealed the asbestos in using a shellac (or another sealer) spray. I cannot say for sure that this works, although I have heard promising reports.

Checking the walls is trickier. They are all sealed (presumably) behind plaster or sheetrock (drywall). Therefore, first turn off the electricity at the main fuse box or circuit breaker box (see Chapter 8). Then go to an exterior wall, and remove the cover plate from an electrical socket box. Now the box and the socket are exposed.

Next comes the tricky part. Usually, when the sheetrock is cut to fit around the socket box, it is cut a bit larger than necessary (to ensure it will fit). There is often a space, perhaps a quarter-wide, at the edge of the electrical socket box that opens directly into the wall. Using a narrow screwdriver, poke around inside that narrow space. If there's insulation, you should be able to feel it easily and even pull out a tiny piece. You can use a small flashlight to look inside and see it. If there's no insulation, try another socket or two. It might be that the insulation is just pulled back from the socket box you tried. If there's no insulation anywhere, the walls probably are not insulated.

Determining whether the floors are insulated requires getting underneath them, either in the crawlspace or in the basement. In the crawlspace, the presence or lack of insulation will be obvious. (Usually, insulation is in the form of "bats," or sheets held in place by thin wires.) The same holds true for insulation in the basement, if the ceiling isn't covered. If it is covered, remove any ceiling fixture (after turning off the power at the main fuse box or circuit breaker box), and use the same technique described above for finding insulation in the walls.

You may also want to check whether the hot and cold water pipes and the heating ducts are insulated. For tips on this, see Chapters 7 and 9.

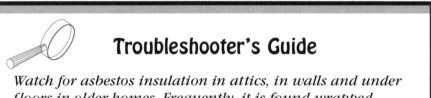

Troubleshooter's Guide

Watch for asbestos insulation in attics, in walls and under floors in older homes. Frequently, it is found wrapped around hot water pipes and heating ducts. If you're not sure, stay away, and let an expert check it out. As noted, removing asbestos can be very expensive.

Finally, look for weatherstripping at doors and windows. Ideally, all exposed edges will be weatherstripped to prevent the loss of heat or the entrance of cold air into the home. Adding weatherstripping is relatively easy and quite effective, and most people can do a reasonably good job themselves.

The R-Rating of Insulation

"R-rating" refers to the ability of a substance to resist the passage of heat. All substances have an R-rating. For example, plywood is often rated about 2.8 per inch. Blown-in cellulose is about 2 to 4 per inch, depending on the type. Fiberglass in batting is about 3 to 3.5 per inch.

As you can see, the R-rating of a particular piece of insulation is determined, in large part, by its thickness. The thicker the material, the better the insulation. As a rule of thumb, if the insulation in an attic is blown-in cellulose and is at least 8 inches thick, it probably is close to R-20 insulation. If it's 12 inches thick, it's closer to R-32. Today, many experts recommend at least R-32 in ceilings where the climate is very hot or cold and at least R-20 in walls and floors.

If the insulation is in bats, the R-rating is usually stamped on them. If the insulation is in the walls, assume that it is the thickness of the wall insulation. If the studs are two-by-fours, the insulation is no more than 3½ inches thick (the actual width of the stud), which usually translates to R-11. If the studs are 6 inches thick, the actual width of the insulation is about 5½ inches, which usually translates closer to R-20.

Insulation of Windows and Doors

Although insulating ceilings, floors and walls is a great way to save on heating and cooling costs, an enormous amount of heat is actually transferred through windows and, to a lesser extent, doors. A typical single pane may have an R-value of only 1. Add another pane, and the window's R-rating goes to 2 to perhaps 4, depending on the quality and type of window. A triple pane should yield an R-rating of 4 to 6 or even higher.

Any home in a hot or cold climate should have at least double-pane windows. Triple-pane is better. If the home has neither, the single-pane windows can be retrofitted. However, it is costly because usually the entire old window and frame must be removed and brand new ones inserted. This usually means breaking some of the exterior covering (such as stucco) and interior wallboard, often requiring replastering, retexturing and repainting of the area. As you can see, it can get complicated and costly. I would value a home lower in hot or cold climates if it did not have at least double-pane windows.

Doors to the outside should all be solid core to be well insulated. (Besides, a hollow-core door provides almost no security against break-ins. Any strong person can kick it down with one well-placed blow.) If it is solid core, check it for weather-stripping, as noted earlier.

Floor Problems

FEW people think of the floors as a separate system in a home, comparable to the plumbing or the wiring. But floors are unique, with concerns associated only with them. This chapter will look at several problems with floors, what causes them and the cost of and options for correcting them.

When inspecting a home's floors, check for the following:

- Squeaks

- Unevenness

- Broken, scratched or loose tiles

- Rotted or soiled carpeting

Squeaks

Most people expect wood floors to squeak a little (this is not a problem found in cement slabs). Over time, the plywood sub-floor tends to separate from the joists beneath it, lifting up here and there. When a person walks on the subfloor, he or she forces it down and a squeak can be heard. This is not uncommon and usually is not a cause for concern.

If the noise is bothersome, there are numerous methods of dealing with it. Screws can sometimes be inserted to hold the subfloor in contact with the joists. If this is impractical, it may be possible to add shims from underneath.

There are, however, a few circumstances where squeaks indicate a more serious problem. Sometimes a foundation will crack and shift, and the floor joists it supports will be pushed and pulled in many directions, causing them to separate from the subfloor. If the squeaks occur in conjunction with foundation problems, have a structural engineer check the situation.

Also, some floors do not use joists supported by a foundation. Rather, they use a pier system, short joists and heavy plywood (2 inches thick). The floor literally floats on the piers. Over time, this type of floor can develop high and low spots (see Figure 12.1 and the next section), which can cause squeaks and even metallic clanking sounds (if pier jacks were used underneath). Usually, a "tuning"—in which a mechanic goes underneath and adjusts the jacks or uses shims on the piers—will correct the problem.

Unevenness

Unevenness is rarely a problem in new homes, but in older homes, particularly where there's a drainage problem, it occurs frequently. How do you tell whether a floor is uneven?

Troubleshooter's Guide

I once bought a home that had a floor that reminded me of waves in an ocean. It was supported by piers, and water had seeped in underneath the floor during winters, then dried out during summers. As a result, some piers were higher, and some, lower. In addition, the flooring itself had warped in a few areas. It cost $2,500 to have professionals adjust the piers and shave the flooring until everything was even.

In another instance, a friend bought a home located on a cut-and-fill lot (see Chapter 3). One end of the lot had slipped, causing a corner of the home to droop. As a result, one corner of the living room floor sagged nearly 2 inches. Correcting the problem required pouring a new foundation and a portion of a new slab. The cost exceeded $9,000.

Figure 12.1 Cutaway View of Home Showing Piers Underneath, Uneven Floors and Ball Rolling to Low Spot

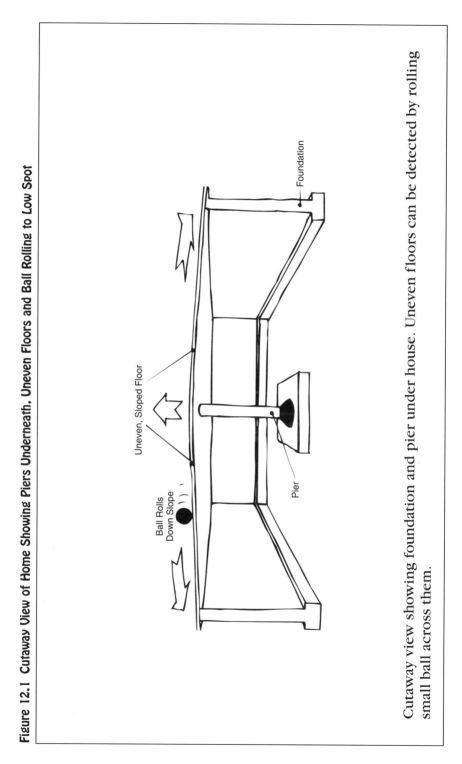

Cutaway view showing foundation and pier under house. Uneven floors can be detected by rolling small ball across them.

Sometimes, if there is a gross displacement, your eye will catch it. One corner of a room may seem lower than another. Or you may actually feel a bump as you walk across the floor. To be sure, try the marble trick. (Note: This does not work well when there is carpeting on the floor. You may have to lift the carpeting to try it.)

Get a large marble or small ball, about 1 inch in diameter, place it in the center of the floor, and see what happens. If the floor is uneven, the marble will roll toward the lowest point. You can check for unevenness by starting the marble at doorways, as well. Sometimes, it may be necessary to give the marble a little push to get it started. If the floor is even, the marble should continue to roll in the direction you push it. If the floor is not even, the marble will turn toward the lowest spot.

I suppose there's nothing terrible about uneven floors. If it doesn't bother you, you can live with them. However, they will affect your ability to get the price you want when you sell. When I'm buying and the floors are uneven, I insist the seller fix them as a condition of the sale.

Broken, Scratched or Loose Tiles

Besides the subfloor, the surface floor can also present problems. When a floor has been tiled, those tiles may be broken, scratched or loose. This is easy to detect simply by observation. One possible way to determine whether a tile is loose is to tap it gently with your foot. If it adheres strongly to the subfloor, it should give a solid sound. If it's loose, it will clank against the subfloor, and the sound will be almost like an echo. Of course, if the grout is loose, you may even be able to pry up a loose tile with your fingers. (Note: Get permission from the owner before attempting to lift any tiles. You could loosen solid tiles in the process.)

If you detect a problem with broken, scratched or loose tiles, determining the cost to fix them can be difficult. If the owner has spare tiles (as is frequently the case), it may simply be a matter of replacing and regrouting. You could do it yourself or hire someone to do it for a nominal cost. However, if no spares exist, it's quite likely that you will find it impossible to match the problem tiles. In that case, the only real solution may be to retile the entire area—something that could be very expensive. Get a bid from a good tile professional.

One additional concern should be why tiles are loose or broken. (Scratching usually comes from not keeping them clean and then walking on them when there was grit present.) Often problem tiles are an indication of a more serious floor problem underneath. See the sections above.

Rotted or Soiled Carpeting

Probably the most common floor problem occurs with wall-to-wall carpeting. These days, it is common to find such carpeting in most homes, and often its appearance will go a long way toward making or breaking a sale.

When inspecting carpeting, remember that all carpeting wears out and that any carpeting that is more than four or five years old will probably need to be replaced fairly soon, particularly if it is soiled or worn. The owner of the property can often tell you fairly accurately how old the carpeting is.

Begin by checking for worn areas on the carpeting, particularly in hallways and entrances. A worn area usually shows as carpeting lying flat or thinned.

The longevity of carpeting depends in large measure on its quality. Today, all sorts of materials and weaves are used. However, pick up a piece of the carpeting (you can usually draw up a corner a few inches, turn it over, then lay it back and kick it down into place), and look at the thickness of the weave (the thicker, the better) and the quality of the backing. A frail backing usually indicates a poor-quality rug.

Soiled carpeting is a different matter. Some dirt and stains can be removed, some cannot; and sometimes the removal process will damage the carpeting. You can't really know how the carpet will look until it's actually cleaned. Most owners, however, have their carpets cleaned prior to putting their homes up for sale. If that's the case, what you see is what you get. Soiled areas that are either lighter or darker than the rest of the carpeting are probably there to stay. The only real way to fix them is to recarpet. Recarpeting a home of about 2,000 square feet could easily cost $5,000 at minimum.

Beware of odors in carpeting, particularly cat and dog urine. (Always ask whether a pet has lived in the home. If so, use your nose to check the carpeting, even if you have to get down on all fours to do it!) Although some carpet cleaners claim they have special chemicals that will remove odors, I have found these to be ineffective. If a carpet has been soiled with urine, about the only way to get rid of the odor is to get new carpeting, new padding and, in some cases, new flooring underneath. Don't underestimate this problem. Even if the odor doesn't appear to be too strong, in winter, when you close the windows and turn up the heat, you might find that the odor wells up out of the carpeting and is strong enough to make your eyes water. You won't want to live in that situation, and the time to do something about it is when you discover the problem upon inspection.

Checking Safety and Security Features

THIS may be the shortest chapter in this book, but it is certainly one of the most important. Every home should have certain safety features. The more the better. Learn what and whether they are in working condition.

On your inspection of a home's safety and security features, check for the following:

- Fire extinguishers

- Smoke alarms

- Distance to nearest fire plug

- Interior sprinkler system

- Locks

- Security system

Fire Extinguishers

There should be an operative ABC fire extinguisher in the kitchen, the utility room and the garage. At discount stores, these sell for about $10 to $15 apiece. ("A" stands for paper, wood and trash; "B," for liquids and grease; and "C," for electrical equipment. Different chemicals are used for each. An ABC extinguisher can handle all three types of fire in the home.)

Smoke Alarm

It should go without saying that there should be at least one operative smoke alarm on each level of the home. If the home is large, more than one may be necessary. Today, in addition to alarms that detect visible smoke, there are alarms available that detect noxious but invisible gases. You may want to consider installing these, as well.

One debate over smoke alarms is whether they should be battery powered or should plug into the 110-volt home current. Building departments differ in their views. Some insist that 110-volt plug-in units be used because they are afraid people will forget to change the battery on the other style. Others insist that the battery units be used because often, in a home fire, the first system to go is the electrical.

To be safe, use a combination. Some combination units are available (ones that plug in *and* use a battery), but they are fairly expensive. On the other hand, you probably can get a plug-in unit and a separate battery unit for less than $20 for both. Better to spend a couple of extra bucks for both than to be sorry you installed only one type.

Distance to Nearest Fire Plug

The distance between the home and the nearest fire plug is something to investigate. If it's more than 400 feet, it could be a problem. You might have to pay more for fire insurance and in the event of a fire, there may be more chance the home will burn down because the fire department won't be able to connect its hoses quickly.

Interior Sprinkler System

Interior sprinkler systems are usually found only on new, expensive homes. The cost of putting in such a system is quite high, and most owners of modestly priced homes cannot afford it. If the home has a fire sprinkler system, it is a definite plus.

(Note: Don't try out the system! There should be a gauge somewhere that will let you know it's pressurized. If you light a match to even one sprinkler head, the entire system might activate, sprinkling the home, the furniture and everyone present. You wouldn't want to explain that to an unhappy owner.)

As well as providing safety, a sprinkler system may reduce the cost of fire insurance significantly.

Locks

These days, security is important. Therefore, all exterior doors should be solid core. Tap on the door if you're not sure. It should sound solid. If it sounds hollow and if the surface veneer can be depressed easily, the door is probably hollow. Almost anyone can knock down a hollow-core door with a few kicks. A solid-core door with at least three hinges, however, can take an enormous beating before it gives.

Each exterior door, in my opinion, should have at least two locks: one standard door lock and one dead bolt. These can be purchased for about $25 apiece, but installing them is tricky.

Windows should also have two locks. Most sliding glass windows have the standard lock or catch that secures the window when it is closed. There should also be a secondary lock—perhaps a metal slide that fits into a hole when the window is in the closed or partially opened position.

Security System

Many homes these days have security systems. These often consist of motion detectors and light sensors. When the system is activated, anyone walking through various rooms or hallways in the home is detected. The system may then set off a loud alarm bell or gong and may automatically send a phone message to a security service. Usually, the service immediately calls the home. If no one answers or if the person who answers cannot give a correct key code, the service alerts the police.

Security systems are a plus, and having one may yield a significant reduction in the cost of homeowner's insurance premiums. However, they are not without problems. You must arm your system when you leave and disarm it when you return. Otherwise, it may go off when you least expect or want it to. Police departments, faced with numerous false alarms from home security systems, often institute a maximum number of free calls. For example, if your alarm system goes off, the police might come to the home up to three times at no cost if they are false alarms. After three times, you might have to pay for every false alarm, which could cost hundreds of dollars.

If the home being inspected has such a system, ask the owner for a demonstration. Also, be sure that the system is covered under a home warranty plan.

Termite Trouble

TERMITES are prevalent in most parts of the country. Their eating habits are the problem. They love wood, and a wood frame home looks like a good meal to them.

This chapter will not go into great detail on how to determine whether a home has termites. The reason is simply that in virtually all real estate transactions involving financing (which is about 99 percent of them), the lender requires a termite clearance. That means a professional termite inspector will check the home not only for termites but for wood-eating ants, dry rot and a host of other potential parasites. Why should you bother to inspect for termites when a professional will do it anyway? Besides, checking for termites is actually quite a tricky and sometimes difficult chore.

The text will cover some alternatives you have when the inspector reports that the home has termites or other similar parasites. Getting rid of them can be expensive, or not so expensive, depending on the option you choose.

When inspecting a home for termites, consider the following questions:

- How is the report to be interpreted?

- Who does the work?

- What options are available?

Troubleshooter's Guide

You don't have to rely on a termite inspector's report or estimate of repair costs. Often the termite inspector is the same person who handles repairs, so there's an inherent risk of conflict of interest. I've had as many as three different termite inspections on the same property when I didn't like the results of the first two. (The repair work suggested and costs of repair differed enormously.) Then I chose who I wanted to do the work. What counts is a termite clearance for the lender and that all reports are made available to both the buyer and the seller.

How Is the Report To Be Interpreted?

Most termite reports that are positive—in other words, that find evidence of infestation—give a small outline of the home, then note where the infestation was found, what kind it was, what's needed to repair it and how much it will all cost.

If infestation is found, you must assume that the report is accurate. It will have to be fixed, usually at the cost of the seller. As noted above, however, different inspectors recommend different methods of treatment, along with widely ranging costs. A seller needs only a clearance, so he or she will almost always choose the cheapest method.

A buyer, however, wants a good job, and therefore, may be willing to pay extra for it. Most reports offer two kinds of repair work. The first is mandatory and must be done to remove the infestation. The second is optional and may be done as preventive work. I have yet to see a seller who will pay for preventive work. But if you're a buyer, you may want to seriously consider it. Keep in mind, however, that it's almost always money out of your own pocket.

Who Does the Work?

It's easiest to have the termite inspector do the repair work. The reason is simple: He or she found the problem; and if the inspector does the work, he or she guarantees to fix it and render a clearance. On the other hand, if someone else does the work (such as the seller), there's the need for (and cost of) a reinspection, with no guarantee the inspector will approve the work.

On the other hand, when the work recommended is removing and replacing boards, replastering and painting (as is the case with old termite infestations or dry rot), it's far cheaper if the owner does it, and many owners will.

From the buyer's perspective, however, this is not always the best choice. The owner may do an acceptable job in terms of correcting the damage, but the work may not look professional. The inspector might pass such a job, but the buyer might not like it. For that reason, it's always a good idea to have a contingency in the deposit receipt stating that the buyer must approve termite work that's done by someone other than a professional. Sellers will not like this clause, but it keeps them on their toes!

What Options Are Available?

There is a broad spectrum of termite problems, from those that occur in the ground around the home to those that occur in the walls and attic. When there's a problem with termites in the ground and the inspector wants to inject chemicals into that ground, the buyer may have few alternatives. To get the clearance, the work may have to be done the way the inspector wants it done.

However, when there's an infestation in the walls or attic, it's a different story. Sometimes only a beam or two need be removed. If that's the case, the solution is easy and usually inexpensive.

Other times, however, the inspector may want the entire home fumigated because it's impossible to get to all the wood that's infested. That's a different story. Tenting an average-size home can cost upwards of $2,000. Normally, the seller pays all, but sometimes the seller limits the amount he or she will pay for a termite clearance in the sales agreement. The seller may simply refuse to pay any more than the stated limit, even if it means he or she loses the sale. In that case, the buyer may be forced to pay if he or she really wants the home.

An alternative to tenting and fumigation has recently come onto the market: freezing. Small holes are bored in the wall near the site of the infestation, and a chemical—frequently liquid nitrogen—is pumped in. This kills the termites and does not require complete tenting. It's also sometimes a quarter of the cost.

The problem is that the freezing solution may burst any water pipes that might be in the wall. This unfortunate consequence occurred when the process was new and drove some dealers into bankruptcy because of resulting lawsuits. More recently, however, experienced companies drain all water from the plumbing system and use other means to protect pipes. Be sure you find a dealer who will guarantee his or her work, perhaps even with a bond.

The home must obtain a termite clearance. However, the cost of that clearance is often up to the buyer and seller. It's a good idea to come together to negotiate costs and quality of work before any work is done. This way, everyone ends up satisfied.

15

Earthquake Retrofitting

IN California, the West and other areas, retrofitting homes to withstand earthquakes is of increasing concern. Legislation is being considered that would require sellers to retrofit homes as a condition of sale. This could be extremely costly. Thus, it's to everyone's advantage to determine as part of an inspection just how earthquake safe a property is. (Note: The same concerns apply to homes in hurricane and cyclone country.)

Before going further, however, it's important to understand that while precautions can be taken, there's nothing that can guarantee that a home will survive an earthquake, especially a strong one. The 1993 Northridge earthquake near Los Angeles proved this beyond a doubt. Freeway bridges that were tied down and built to withstand lateral earthquake pressure collapsed when the ground literally jumped up and down. Just because a home has been earthquake retrofitted does not mean it is completely secure.

Furthermore, if you're concerned about earthquake safety for the home you are inspecting, contact a competent contractor who can inform you of regulations and procedures currently in effect in your area.

When examining a home for earthquake retrofitting, determine the existence of the following (see Figure 15.1):

Figure 15.1 Wall Showing Diagonal Bracing, Stud Spacing, and Foundation and Roof Tie-Downs

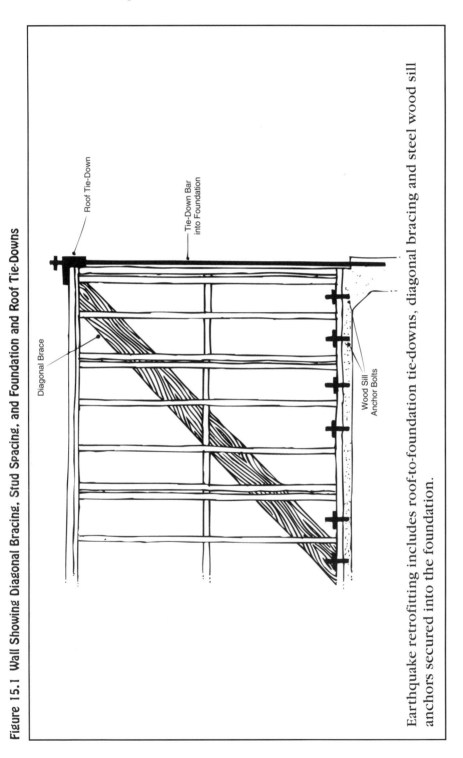

Roof Tie-Down

Tie-Down Bar into Foundation

Diagonal Brace

Wood Sill Anchor Bolts

Earthquake retrofitting includes roof-to-foundation tie-downs, diagonal bracing and steel wood sill anchors secured into the foundation.

- Diagonal Bracing
- Study spacing
- Foundation tie-downs
- Steel roof tie-downs

Diagonal Bracing

Diagonal bracing may be the single most important factor when it comes to earthquake protection. Homes are usually built with rectangular walls. To demonstrate the effectiveness of this construction, form a rectangle out of a drinking straw and push on any side. You'll see that it easily collapses. Now, using the same straw, form a triangle. Triangles, when pushed, do not collapse (although they can break). Thus, to prevent a wall of a home from collapsing during the stress of an earthquake, a diagonal brace (forming a triangle) is usually installed. This is a piece of wood run diagonally across the wall and actually cut into the studs. (Sometimes metal is used, nailed on each stud.)

Check in the garage and in any exposed wall to see that this sort of bracing is present. There should be at least one diagonal brace for every exterior wall, more if the wall has a long run. If bracing is not present, it should be added.

Sometimes, instead of diagonally, plywood is nailed horizontally across the studs. As long as the plywood is at least 5/8 of an inch thick, is nailed every 3 or 4 inches with 3-inch nails and covers many studs, it can also give good support.

Stud Spacing

In most homes with wood studs (vertical support boards, as opposed to the metal studs now gaining popularity), the studs are placed every 16 inches. In some parts of the country, however, to make housing more affordable, the spacing has been increased, often to 2 feet or 3 feet.

The problem is that in many cases, particularly for outside walls, the studs support the roof. When an earthquake, a hurricane or a cyclone occurs and stress is placed across the home, studs positioned too far apart can collapse, bringing down the home. Check in the garage and exposed areas that the studs are no more than 16 inches apart. If they are spaced more widely, I would insist on a structural report on the home.

Troubleshooter's Guide

Sometimes homes are built with a "cripple." This is a short wall between the foundation and the first floor. While the home itself may have diagonal bracing, oftentimes these cripples don't and, as a consequence, are the first to fail in a stress situation. Nailing plywood to them, as described above, is a common method of retrofitting.

Foundation Tie-Downs

In the Loma Prieta earthquake of 1989, much of the damage done in San Francisco was due to the fact that older homes simply sat on their foundations without being tied directly to them. When the earthquake hit, the buildings bounced off the foundations and collapsed.

Determine that the home is, indeed, tied down to its foundation. You can usually check this in the garage or under the home.

Being tied down means that steel rods come up from the cement of the foundation and go through the wood sill (the piece of wood that lies on the foundation and to which the studs are attached), then are secured with washers and bolts. The rods are typically placed every 2 to 3 feet at a minimum around the periphery of the home. If the home is not tied down, it is possible to retrofit these rods. Holes can be drilled into the concrete, special expansion bolts fitted and these screwed down on the sill. You can do this yourself, although it is probably a project for an expert. (Note: The holes for the bolts in the concrete should be *drilled,* not forced with an impact hammer. Drilling takes longer and is more expensive, but the impact hammer can break the concrete, particularly if the concrete is old.)

(Note: In addition to being tied down to the foundation, the home should be fitted with special steel bracing on all support beams underneath and throughout the home. This keeps these supports together when the building shakes and wobbles.)

Roof Tie-Downs

Recent high-tech analysis of homes that have undergone severe earthquakes has suggested that a superior method of tying down a roof (to be used in addition to, not in place of, those mentioned earlier) is to tie down the top sill of the home and lock in the roof with steel clips. Essentially, a steel rod is fastened to the foundation at each corner, then goes up to the top sill of the roof and is fastened there. This helps force the walls to remain in place, no matter how hard the ground shakes. If the roof is likewise fastened with steel braces or clips, it too can't move. This procedure can be retrofitted on an existing home; however, some of the steel may be visible from either the outside or the inside.

16

The April/ October Home Checkup

HOME inspection shouldn't be limited to only those times when you are buying or selling a property. You should inspect your home on a regular basis to catch problems before they get out of control. For example, it's easier to fix a few shingles that blow off than to wait until water soaks through the ceiling, walls, furniture and carpeting.

Although maintenance can be ongoing and handled monthly, sometimes it's easier if you establish specific times of the year to handle it. Therefore, I'm suggesting a fall/spring schedule. Fall means you might want to check the property on October 1st or thereabouts. Spring might be April 1st.

I suggest that the first thing you do is simply walk around the outside of the home, then each room inside, and look for anything out of the ordinary. If you see something obvious, like a black burned stain by a socket or a broken gutter, check it out and have it fixed. Otherwise, work your way through the easy ten-point check list in Figure 16.1.

Figure 16.1 Spring/Fall Checklist

❏   Check the roof. (Fall)
    Look for loose shingles, exposed areas where shingles
    have blown away, branches or other items lying on the
    roof.
❏   Check the gutters. (Fall)
    Clean out any leaves that have collected in the gutters,
    and make sure the downspouts work. Look for broken,
    loose or rotted gutters or downspouts.
❏   Trim the trees. (Fall and spring)
    Trees that grow close to the home can drop branches
    and leaves on the roof, damaging it or the gutter system.
    In hot summer months, trees growing close to the home
    can present a serious fire danger. Trim them back.
❏   Check for foundation cracks. (Fall and spring)
    In the winter, water entering tiny foundation cracks can
    expand and lengthen them, eventually leading to a
    broken foundation. In the spring, small weeds growing
    in the cracks can do the same thing. Patch all
    foundation cracks inside and out.
❏   Change the furnace filter. (Fall and spring)
    Ideally, the furnace filter should be changed once a
    month, year round if the home has air-conditioning.
    However, most people put this off or forget about it.
    Therefore, change it at least twice a year.
❏   Check the weatherstripping. (Fall and spring)
    In the spring, replace storm windows and doors with
    screens. In the fall, check the weatherstripping around
    all doors and windows. Over time, it can fall off or
    decay.
❏   Paint. (Fall and spring)
    Most people think of paint as simply decorative. But it
    actually protects the material beneath, particularly if it's
    wood. If the paint is peeling, it's probably time to put
    on another coat. Not only will the home look better, but
    the wood underneath will retain its freshness.
❏   Clean the fireplace. (Fall)
    At least once a year, hire a chimney sweep to clean the
    fireplace. The cost is frequently less than $100—well
    worth it to avoid the possibility of fire.

Figure 16.1 Spring/Fall Checklist (Continued)

❏   Test the electrical circuits. (Fall and spring)
Trip and reset all circuit breakers to ensure that they
still operate and to keep them from getting plugged.
Also, check any sockets, switches or fixtures that don't
work, and replace them, as needed.

❏   Check for leaks. (Fall and spring)
Check all spigots inside and out for leaks, and replace
washers, as necessary. This could save you a lot on your
water bill. Also, check for leaks in the traps under sinks
and at the bottom of the water heater. (Be sure the
water heater's vent is intact and in place.)

17

Pool and Spa Checks

THE pool and spa require a special inspection and usually a special inspector. Pool service companies can often refer you to a pool inspection company. These are in business to check pools for leaks and other problems and are often called upon at times other than when a home is sold. Their rates are reasonable, and I strongly suggest using them, as they can perform specific tests on pools (such as using colored water to determine the extent of a leak) that you can't do easily and that can reveal a great deal of information.

You can, however, learn a lot about a pool or spa yourself with a little preparation. This chapter will consider the main points of inspection.

When examining a pool, look for the following:

- Improper operation

- Algae

- Faulty equipment

- Cracks and leaks

Improper Operation A swimming pool consists of more than just a hole in the ground filled with water. It also has a filtration system to keep the water clean and a pump to circulate the water.

It may have underwater lights, as well as air jets (if a spa is attached to the pool).

Several types of filters exist. Probably the most common is the diatomaceous earth filter. Here, filter elements (which look like tiny lungs and are made of special filtration cloth) are coated with diatomite. Pool water is then forced through, and dirt and debris are caught on the elements. This system works very well, except that over time, the elements get clogged. One method of cleaning them is to backwash the filter, which reverses the flow of water and pushes the dirt and some diatomite out. Another more thorough method of cleaning is to open the filter canister and clean each element individually with a hose.

A less effective cleaning system is the porous cartridge filter in a tank. Because it is less effective, the system usually needs much more filter area than does a diatomaceous earth system. Cartridge filters are normally used in spas, rarely in larger pools. To clean the filter, remove it, then spray it with a strong stream of water.

Finally, the sand filter traps dirt in layers of sand. Like the diatomaceous filter, it too must be cleaned regularly, usually by backwashing.

In addition to the filters is an electric pump motor and a pump, plus pipes that connect the entire system. As part of your inspection, I strongly urge you to have the owner demonstrate the operation of the system. You should, at minimum, see the following:

- The equipment should be operated on the normal filter cycle. Water should enter the filter system from the main drain and the skimmer, returning to the pool via outlets. Put your hand over the return outlets, and try to close them off. There should be strong pressure there. Also, the water should look clean coming out. If the water is dirty or there is little pressure, the filter may need to be backwashed or cleaned. That could suggest problems with dirt and algae (to be covered shortly) in the pool.

- The same equipment, with the addition of a long hose, pole and vacuum head, is used to clean the pool. Have the owner demonstrate that the vacuum system works. It should readily suck up dirt and small debris from the deepest part of the pool.

- To clean the system, assuming it's diatomaceous earth or sand, the system must backwash. Have the owner demonstrate the backwash cycle. (Note: Backwashing produces a kind of grey-white sludge as the scum from inside the filter is sent out. Check whether there is a trap to catch this. Letting it flow unrestricted onto the streets is prohibited in some locales.)

- Have an electrician or a pool expert inspect any lighting. Be careful! Sometimes in older pools, the grounding for lights has failed, and they could discharge electricity directly into the water. If you're not sure, have the lights completely disconnected from any electrical service.

Algae   Most people think of pools as extensions of a mountain lake or even the ocean. A more correct, though far less flattering, analogy would be that of a toilet. The pool is a limited body of water that constantly has debris falling into it (including skin and dirt particles from swimmers) and will quickly stagnate if it is not constantly cleaned.

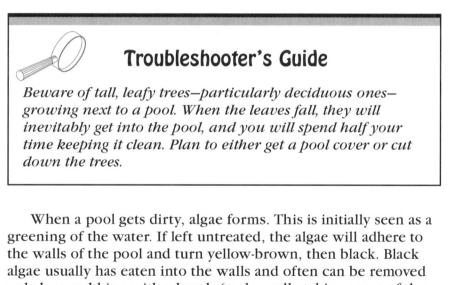

Troubleshooter's Guide

Beware of tall, leafy trees—particularly deciduous ones— growing next to a pool. When the leaves fall, they will inevitably get into the pool, and you will spend half your time keeping it clean. Plan to either get a pool cover or cut down the trees.

When a pool gets dirty, algae forms. This is initially seen as a greening of the water. If left untreated, the algae will adhere to the walls of the pool and turn yellow-brown, then black. Black algae usually has eaten into the walls and often can be removed only by scrubbing with a brush (and usually taking some of the plaster with it) and using an acid wash. Don't think that algae is inconsequential. It is a serious problem.

The usual method of controlling algae is to treat the pool with chlorine, after acid-balancing the water. Also, the filtration system must function well so that organic particles are removed from the water, denying the algae substances on which to feed.

Troubleshooter's Guide

I once bought a property where the previous owner had let the maintenance lapse on the pool. Black algae covered its walls. Ultimately, I had to have the pool walls sandblasted, then replastered, because the algae had gotten so ingrained in the walls it couldn't be completely removed. Never underestimate the importance of having a clean pool.

Ideally, a pool will have bright, clear, blue water. Green water is a bad sign. Yellow, brown or black spots on the sides of the pool indicate a progressively worse problem with algae. My suggestion is that if you are a buyer, insist that the pool be cleaned before you buy the property. The owner may simply be unaware of the extent of the problem, until he or she goes to fix it.

Faulty Equipment   Once the pool is in the ground, the most expensive repairs usually (but not always) are to the equipment. This includes the filter, pump, drains and pipes. Let's take them one at a time.

The filter rarely breaks, but the container (sometimes made of stainless steel, other times plastic) may rust, get holes in it and leak. In addition, if there's a canister or filter elements inside, these can deteriorate or rip and must be replaced. A complete new filter can cost hundreds of dollars.

Ideally, to inspect a filter, you need to have it broken down so you can see inside. If you can see only the outside, check for leaks and (if it's metal) rust marks. Determine that the mounts aren't broken. Operate the pump to see whether any diatomaceous earth comes out of the return (indicating a bad filter element). These are, of course, only superficial checks. The only way to really judge its condition is to have the filter cracked open so you can see inside. You may want to have a professional do this for you.

The pump has two parts: the water pump itself and the motor. Pumps are notorious for burning out. The reason is that they need to be constantly filled with water for cooling. However, sometimes, particularly in an old system, the pump will suck air for a time before it begins operation, and this can quickly burn it out. Check for noise. A pump (and motor) should operate quietly. Any noise probably indicates bad bearings. (Note: An electric motor may give no indications of problems, then, suddenly, without warning, simply quit. If the motor is more than a few years old, assume it will go soon. A new pump and motor [if the pump is plastic] can usually be purchased for about $300, plus installation.)

Drains are of particular concern. Pools usually have two: a skim, located at the surface, and the main drain, located at the deepest part of the pool. The skimmer rarely gives trouble, although its plastic elements sometimes deteriorate. They can usually be replaced at a nominal cost.

The main drain at the bottom of the pool, however, is a different story. This drain is used to get most of the dirt out of the pool. It is also often the best drain for circulating the water and getting proper filtration. However, over time, due to the shifting of earth and the weight of the pool, the pipes connecting this drain may leak or crack, often right at the bottom. When this happens, you have two options, close the drain (thereby making it more difficult to clean the pool and to get good circulation) or continue to pump and lose water. If the leak is small, this won't matter much. However, I once had a friend whose pool had a major leak in its main drain and could lose a foot of water an hour by pumping through it!

Some pool services claim they can fix a main drain problem. However, I'm not sure it's possible. Most of the repairs involve draining the pool, cutting a hole in the bottom and putting in new pipe. The trouble is, in the process, the bottom may be weakened so that the patch, or the drain, may leak again in the future. Another repair involves inserting new plastic pipe into the drain, but I've not seen this process actually done. Yet another method involves draining the pool, then digging down from the outside going underneath until you're right below the drain, then fixing it. The hole is then backfilled with a special compound to prevent shrinkage. In general, if a pool's main drain has problems, the prospects are not good.

Troubleshooter's Guide

Beware of draining pools. During the dry season, and if there is a low ground water table, draining a pool is not a problem. However, if it has rained recently and the water table is high, the pool may act like a boat and, when drained, actually float up! I saw this happen once; the pool popped nearly 2 feet out of the ground. Needless to say, the only remedy at that point was to destroy the pool and put in a new one. Be very careful, and get expert opinion before you drain a swimming pool.

Cracks and Leaks   Finally, there's the matter of cracks and leaks. If the pool is old, it probably has copper pipes. Copper, as noted earlier, is excellent for home water delivery. However, it is not necessarily good for pools. The acid used to stabilize a pool can react with the copper pipe and cause it to thin and eventually develop holes. I've seen copper pool pipes that had so many holes they looked like swiss cheese. Often these pipes leak underground, where it's difficult to find and patch the holes. PVC pipe is far better for pools. If an old pool has copper pipe, you can pretty well count on leaks eventually occurring. You might consider the cost of switching to plastic.

Pools can also leak through the concrete. Cracks can develop over time as the pool settles into the ground. Ground shifting can add to the problem.

As a pool ages, some cracking of the surface plaster is normal and may not be a problem (other than cosmetic). However, if the crack goes through the concrete and the pool leaks, it's a serious problem.

Usually, but not always, you can see cracks. If you are concerned, a pool testing service can spread a dye in the pool water in front of a crack and check outside to see whether the dye comes through, thus determining the extent of the crack. Of course, this works only with cracks near the water surface. Other detection methods are used for cracks on the bottom of the pool.

Most cracks in the cement and the plaster can be patched, assuming the pool was built correctly, with an adequate amount of steel reinforcement. The cost, however, varies significantly. Get estimates from several contractors if you are worried about this.

Also, check decks and coping for cracks. Cement ground covering all around the pool extending out for at least 3 feet is not merely cosmetic. It helps to direct water that is splashed out of the pool away from the ground directly around it. Helping to keep that ground dry goes a long way to avoiding shifts that can crack the pool.

Troubleshooter's Guide

Often the decking around the pool comes right up to the edge and then there's space before the pool itself starts. This space is usually filled with a compound such as Deck-O-Seal, which can expand and contract with temperature changes and can provide a secure seal. It does, however, wear out over time and may need to be replaced. It could cost a $100 or more to have this seal replaced.

Spas

All rules that apply to the maintenance of pools, especially keeping the water clean, also apply to spas. However, most spas these days are made of fiberglass and, if installed properly, rarely leak, rust or crack.

The biggest problem I have found is that people tend to ignore maintenance on a spa. That coupled with high water temperatures often results in algae growth or foul-smelling water. Adding appropriate amounts of chlorine or bromine and acid-balancing the water usually takes care of such problems. However, see the section above if there's algae in the spa.

A spa must always have a cover. The solid plastic-core covers that are about 3 inches thick are best, although floating plastic bubble covers will work. Covers keep out leaves and dirt, and they help maintain a high water temperature without wasting energy.

In addition to inspecting the pump and filter (usually two cartridge filters are used), be sure to check the spa's heater. It should be able to warm the water to at least 102 degrees within a reasonable amount of time and maintain the temperature. Spas that are self-contained and electrically heated can sometimes cost $100 a month or more to heat, especially in winter. Gas or even solar heating, once installed, is far less expensive.

How To Find a Good Home Inspector

YES, you can do it all yourself. But, if you're unfamiliar with home building, some of the checks suggested in this book may seem foreign to you. Therefore, my suggestion is that you consider hiring a competent professional home inspector to accompany you on the day you inspect the home. If there's a problem, you may want to hire a specialist such as a soil or structural engineer. And you'll surely want to have a termite inspector examine the property.

The idea is to work *with* these professionals. If you're a buyer, their expertise can help you to better determine the true condition of the property. In addition, they can often suggest remedies that neither you nor the owner may have considered.

How To Find a Competent Home Inspector

Home inspection is a relatively new industry and, thus far, is not well regulated. Most states are considering regulating home inspectors, but many have not yet done so. Even those that have, often require only that inspectors pass rudimentary tests. The truth is that in many areas today, almost anyone, including you or me, can hang out a shingle and call himself or herself a home inspector. That's changing but perhaps not fast enough for you. Therefore, if you want a competent inspector, how do you find one?

Inspectors are listed in the yellow pages of the phone book under Home Inspection Services or something similar. However, picking an inspector out of the phone book is like choosing a restaurant—you don't know what you're really getting until it's too late.

ASHI

A growing association called the American Society of Home Inspectors has some minimum qualifications, as well as ethics requirements, for its members. I would think membership in ASHI should be a minimum for your home inspector.

Recommendations

In addition, I would ask the following people and organizations for recommendations:

- Brokers (buyers' and sellers'). They use inspectors regularly and often can recommend one to you.

- Building and safety departments. Sometimes home inspectors are retired from local building departments. These are the people who regularly inspect property for the city to be sure it meets codes. Hiring one of these professionals as your inspector couldn't hurt.

- Contractors. Although contractors often get business referrals from inspectors, a potential conflict of interest, they often will recommend inspectors and may know those who are really good. Get recommendations from several contractors.

If, after checking the above sources, you find the same name popping up over and over, you may have a winner. Call the inspector, and interview him or her.

Interviewing the Home Inspector

At a minimum, before hiring an inspector, I would ask for his or her credentials. (For example, did the inspector work in the building department? Is he or she a licensed contractor? In what area? Does the inspector have an engineering degree?)

I would also ask for the names of at least three people whose homes he or she has inspected in the past six months. This should be easy to supply, and if the inspector won't, ask yourself why? Then I would call each of those people. Find out how the inspection went. Were they satisfied? Did something later turn up that the inspector overlooked?

Hiring the Inspector

Home inspections run between $250 and $450. The inspection itself frequently takes only two or three hours, and a quick inspector can get in three homes a day. As you can see, there's a lot of money to be made. Once you hire an inspector, you're committed to the inspection and the fee. If you don't like the inspection, complain. Sometimes an adjustment can be made.

Accompanying the Inspector

If you hire a home inspector, then don't accompany him or her on the inspection tour, you're getting only half your money's worth. The written report (described below) may not even touch on the variety of information you could get by being there and asking questions. In addition, a good inspector will point out things as he or she goes along. Sometimes this dialogue will be the best part of the inspection, providing information and insight you couldn't otherwise get. For example, you might not understand what the inspector means when he says that the vents underneath are plugged. If you're along with the inspector, however, he or she will show you.

When you accompany the inspector, be prepared to rough it. Wear clothes that are warm and can get dirty because you'll crawl over and under things.

The inspector should likewise be appropriately dressed and should carry a tool kit including a light, a screwdriver and an electrical tester. The inspector should inspire confidence, asking appropriate questions of the owner. He or she should also be able to help you verify whether additions have been made with a permit.

The Inspection Report

You will want a written report of the inspection. If you're a buyer, you can use this report to point out problems to the seller and, perhaps, get an adjustment on the price. If you're a seller, you'll want this report to demonstrate to the buyer that you've done an arm's-length inspection, and nothing—except what's noted—was found wanting in the home.

The problem with most reports, however, is that they are computer generated. Several programs are available that will spew out a report after an inspector types in a minimum of information. Therefore, unless the inspector is very conscientious and writes specific comments, one report will look much like another. They tend to be general and, because of that, not very helpful. Indeed, you'll find that a great deal of the report is devoted to a disclaimer by the inspector concerning anything that he or she failed to find.

I don't like computer-generated reports. I want to see the inspector write down by hand what he or she found in great detail. If it takes the inspector an extra half-hour to do so, that's okay; he or she is getting paid quite well. I usually insist up front that I want a "literal" report—that is, a written report. If the inspector wants to use a computer program, that's okay, but there had better be plenty of sheets at the end with his specific comments.

Inspector's Warranties and Liabilities

Because we live in an overly litigious society, inspectors are very wary of lawsuits. This has happened plenty of times, usually because the inspector failed to point out something that the buyer later discovered. The buyer, subsequently, sued the inspector for negligence.

Inspectors, presumably, are liable for their errors, omissions and outright mistakes. However, to cover themselves, they sometimes hedge on questions and never really give a straight answer.

"Is the foundation bad?" you ask. "Well," the inspector may say or write, "it has some cracks that could be serious or superficial. They could get worse or stay the same. You should have the foundation checked by an engineer to be sure." In other words, the inspector covers himself or herself.

As a result, what you often get on an inspection report is a lot of banalities and superficial comments about items and conditions that you could have seen for yourself. On the other hand, if there is a bad condition that's obvious, most inspectors will note it as such. For example, a deck that's about to collapse because the underpinnings have been worn away will probably be noted and warned against by the inspector.

Most inspectors warrant the home only at the time of the inspection. The report will indicate that the conditions noted are accurate only as of the writing of the report. Of course, things could be considerably different by tomorrow.

The truth of the matter is that many home inspectors are retired building inspectors, contractors or engineers. They are competent and strive to do a good job. Work with them, accompany them, ask questions and you should learn a lot.

Appendix
Tools You Will Need

IN order to conduct a home inspection (with or without a professional inspector), you'll need certain tools. These aren't expensive, and chances are you already have them around the house. Be sure that before you begin the inspection tour, you have these available. It's awkward to have to stop an inspection half way through to run to the hardware store for something you forgot.

1. Proper attire (clothes, shoes and hat that can get dirty)
2. Flashlight with extra batteries
3. Long, thin flathead screwdriver
4. Large marble
5. Short carpenter's level
6. Tape measure
7. Binoculars (optional)
8. Small mirror (for seeing behind things)
9. Electrical circuit tester
10. Clipboard to hold paperwork

Index